The way of the Buddha
Is the path of enlightenment
Through self-knowledge—
Knowledge of every aspect of the self,
What the self is,
What the self is not.
When the soul surveys existence and existences—
The round of karma created by desire,
The round of pleasure
Experienced through the physical senses—
And yearns for something more than all of this,
Something within called the eternal bliss,
The soul is ready for the path of the Buddha;
And the Buddha comes quietly.

# Quietly Comes the Buddha

## Books by the Ascended Masters and Their Messengers

# Quietly Comes the Buddha

*By Gautama Buddha ∾ Lord of the World
to the Messenger Elizabeth Clare Prophet*

*Quietly Comes the Buddha*
Published by
THE SUMMIT LIGHTHOUSE
for Church Universal and Triumphant
Box A
Colorado Springs, Colorado 80901

LIBRARY OF CONGRESS CATALOG CARD NUMBER: 76-28087
INTERNATIONAL STANDARD BOOK NUMBER: 0-916766-18-7

Printed in the United States of America

Summit University Press
First Printing

Sons and Daughters of the Ancient of Days,

I write to you as a devotee of the Christ and the Buddha and of the flames of East and West. In this life I was first a lover of God, then a disciple of Christ, and later a devotee of the Buddha. My inner experiences with the Christ and the Buddha revealed to me the essential flame of God the Father in heaven and God the Mother on earth and myself a worshiper in the midst of that flame.

It was then that I knew the responsibility of Mother to feed the children of the Father. And so I applied to the enlightened ones—the ascended masters—to teach me the teaching of the law that I might give it as soul nourishment to the spiritually impoverished evolutions of earth.

My application was received by the ascended master El Morya who was, I discovered, my beloved guru, and by Saint Germain who anointed me as a messenger for the ascended masters in the Aquarian age. Thus for almost two decades I have with my twin flame, the Messenger Mark L. Prophet, set forth the writings of the law of God and the communications of the Lord's hosts.

In 1975, Lord Gautama Buddha came quietly to my soul to deliver to me the teachings on the Ten Perfections of the Law presented in this book as the poetry of his heart's communion with the One. And to mark his coming, he arranged to have sent to me on his birthday, May 8, the 300-year old, life-sized statue of the Buddha which devotees have photographed to include with this book.

The joy of his coming was indescribable. It was the bliss of communion with the All. I was like a child jumping up and down in the excitement of seeing Father after a long separation. He is friend and teacher, companion and confidante. He sits beside me in contemplation of the One. He is adorable!

And the joy of receiving his message was as great as the joy of his coming. The sentences were dictated word by word as the great sphere of awareness that is the mind of the Buddha merged with the sphere of my own higher consciousness and the distillations of the message, drop by drop, were translated sphere to sphere, spiral by spiral, line upon line, precept upon precept for our understanding in time and space. In a different plane, at a different point of time and space, the same teaching of the Buddha is translated out of the original Word into other words and other cadences; for the spherical consciousness of the mind of the Buddha is delivered simultaneously to all evolutions in the planes of Mater and to each disciple according to his evolution and to his understanding.

The teaching is universally applicable. Its many facets are always in harmony with the whole and with the law of the One. All argument concerning doctrine and dogma is only the result of differing testimony of the same universal law by those of varying frequencies, hence varying degrees of perspective of the mind of Christ and the mind of Buddha.

In these letters from the Lord of the World, you will find the unifying factor of the Spirit of Life which undergirds all true science and true religion. As I received these messages and penned them with joy for the children of God on earth, the Lord of the World took me into his heart even as he filled my soul. And he showed me the place on the mount of attainment where there is the meeting of the Buddhas and the Christs of the ages, the avatars, prophets, and messengers of God. There were Jesus, Moses, and Elijah, Mohammed, Confucius, Lord Maitreya, the Mother of the East and the Mother of the West, and countless others with their followers.

And I saw, moment by moment, the mind of God meeting the mind of man. I saw Universal Love consuming by the sacred fire all doctrinal division and social schism—the pitting of brother against brother and man against man. I saw death swallowed up in the victory of the law of the One. And I saw the children of God reunited once again after the long dark night of ignorance was banished by the coming of the Son of the eternal Presence, personified in the many incarnations of the sons and daughters of God.

I have set forth these teachings as a disciple of the Buddha and as a representative of the World Mother. With Lord Gautama, I dedicate them to the soul of humanity and to you who are discovering your own Christic and Buddhic identity as a son, a daughter of the Ancient of Days.

I look forward to greeting you on the path of your soul's initiation in the light of the eternal God.

ELIZABETH CLARE PROPHET

Ashram of the World Mother
Los Angeles, California

# Contents

# 1. Becoming the Buddha

# Chelas Ever Mounting
# the Path of Attainment:

There are some
Who are born to be the Christ
And there are some
Who are born to be the Buddha.
Who is Christ?
Who is Buddha?
Who are you?
Why were you born?
To be man, to be woman,
To be father, to be mother.
Yes, this and more.

To be the Christ
Or to be the Buddha where you are,
You must know that that is the goal of life for you.
There are those who know from within,
For their souls have cried out
And they have heeded the call of conscience,
Of inner flame.
They have known with an inner knowing
That this life was intended to be
A victorious manifestation
Of the life everlasting.

At that moment
When the inner and the outer man merge
With the God-realization
That God and only God is the goal of life,
Of evolution, of all effort, human and divine—
At that moment
The spark of the Logos ignites the flame,
The all-consuming passion of the chela [1]
In search of the teacher and the teaching.
Hence the vision of the goal
Inspires the soul
To determine ways and means
Of attaining the goal.
Thus the Eightfold Path was born [2]
Out of my communion
With the Most High God—
A communion that was a supreme compassion,
A deep desire to show mankind
How to return to the center of God-reality
In which I found myself immersed.

O flaming Presence of the Central Sun,
O flaming Reality, thou Cosmic One,
O God, the All-in-all,
How can I impart the quickening, the awakening,
The awareness of the Enlightened One,
To those here below
Who have never tasted of the immortal fount,
Who have not stood with Christ
On transfiguration's mount,
Who have not beheld
The hand of God on Horeb's height
Or borne witness to Elijah's flight,
To those who have not known thyself
In bodhisattva's grace
Or in the eyes of arhat, adept, avatar?

To those who would return to thee
Yet have not glimpsed eternity
I would bring the light,
I would bring the remembrance
Of an origin so vast.
I would bring a cup of living flame
From the altar of the Most High God.
I would offer the cup of liquid gold
To those who honor thee and would hold
Thy light, thy being,
And the cycling of thy law
In mind and heart and soul,
That they might reach the goal.
I give my life, my energy,
For the fusion of humanity
With sacred fire, with mind of God,
With love compelling and wisdom telling
That the way, the Eightfold Path,
Is the means of cycling
To the center of the sun of God consciousness
And the way made plain.
Neither for the proud nor the profane
Is the way of selflessness,
Desirelessness, all-inclusiveness.

I AM the Buddha come again.
I AM the Buddha come to win
Souls for God, for hierarchy,[3]
Souls for freedom, for individuality.
I AM the Buddha.

I come quietly as all-pervasive awareness
Of gentleness, of sweet caress,
Of God enfolding life with tenderness,
A thousand petals of a thousand-petaled rose
And of a lotus that blooms and grows
In the swampland of life—
Symbol of alchemy,
Of transmutation of karma,[4]
Of life transcending cycles
Of pain and suffering.
As point by point the petals of the law
Reveal a soul without flaw,
Redemption's fires in Holy Spirit,
There transpires the purging and the pummeling,
The testing and the tempering
Of a soul that is born to be
The Christ, the Buddha,
To be free.
I AM the Buddha.
I come quietly.

Bidden by the Darjeeling Council
Of the Great White Brotherhood,[5]
I come to tutor those who would be teachers.
I come to take the chelas of East and West,
To take them by the hand
And lead them to Mount Everest.
High in the Himalayas we shall stand—
Your hand in mine and mine in thine.

We hold the hand of hierarchy.
So learn from me, if you will,
Of the chain of hierarchy,
Of worlds within and worlds beyond,
Of galaxies of light,
Of brothers and sisters you have known,
Now a part of cosmic consciousness.
They know where the doves have flown.

The path of the Buddha
Is also the way of the Holy Spirit—
Of caduceus rising
And fourfold mastery of planes of consciousness.
The way of the Buddha
Is the adoration of the Mother.
It is the child adoring the Mother,
The Mother adoring the child.
It is God enveloping man
And man enveloping God,
The Lover and the beloved fused as one life
Even as the Knower becomes the known
And the known becomes the Knower.
I would teach you of wholeness,
Of God as one and of God as twin flames,
Of God as one and God as three-in-one,
Of God as one and God as four,
And on and on,
Until God, as numberless numbers,
Transcends all numbers
And becomes the Infinite One.
Infinity born again and again in you
Is God realized through and through.

I come that you might experience God
As I have done,
So that in passing the torch
Of illumination to the age
Into the keeping of the Mother,
As I have entrusted it to her care,
You might also transfer,
With the torch of illumination,
Illumined action, enlightenment,
And the experience of being God.
Let enlightenment in this age
Be the experience of the Buddha where you are.
Let wisdom be the divining rod of love.
Let all that you are told
Of life and law and liberty
Be that which you now hold
As action, interaction, experience that is proof—
A proof of science and of truth,
A proof that shows in eyes that shine for God
And in a face transparent
With image of Cosmic Virgin smiling through.

Let enlightenment be souls that are free,
Souls winning God-mastery.
Let enlightenment be the mark
Of those who love and keep on loving still
In the face of adversity
And every thrust of tyrant's will.

Let enlightenment be the love
That consumes the dragon in his lair,
Whose rushing, crystal stream
Flowing on to roaring waterfall of light
Drowns out the screaming and the screeching
Of the denizens of night.
Let enlightenment be God-government,
God-vision, and God-victory
For a planet and a people.

I AM the Buddha.
I come quietly.
Let the chelas of Morya listen well,[6]
For I have a tale of attainment to tell.
Week by week I shall unfold
The glory of your becoming sevenfold—
Masters of the sacred law
And possessors of the forces ten.
Listen well, for I shall tell
The story of becoming
The Buddha where you are.


I AM

*Gautama*

in the flame of peace

# 2. The Wheel of Perfection

# Chelas Now Mounting
# the Wheel of Perfection:

The story of Sumedha
Is the story of a soul becoming the Buddha—
Your soul, my soul.
When in the course of the endless cycles
Of human incarnations
The soul begins to ponder the miseries
Attendant upon the wheel of rebirth,
Its subjection to birth and death,
Disease and decay,
By and by it comes to the realization
That peripheral existence is vain[1]—
An endless succession of vanities.

At the end of the chain of miseries,
There is born one day within the soul
The God-determination to be free.
It is then and only then
That the soul pursues the center of the law of cycles,
The origin of being,
And centers itself within the Flaming One.

The way of the Buddha
Is the path of enlightenment
Through self-knowledge—
Knowledge of every aspect of the self,
What the self is,
What the self is not.
When the soul surveys existence and existences—
The round of karma created by desire,
The round of pleasure
Experienced through the physical senses—
And yearns for something more than all of this,
Something within called the eternal bliss,
The soul is ready for the path of the Buddha;
And the Buddha comes quietly.

Mankind have sought escape,
Surcease from sorrow,
And to break the confines of the flesh;
But few have succeeded in retaining an identity,
In securing the destiny of the soul,
Without perfection as the goal.
As long as men have sought
The answers to life in relativity,
They have subjected themselves to laws of mortality.
Self-made and self-imposed are these laws,
And mankind have become a law unto themselves.

By ignoring the inner law of life,
They have gone round and round
In endless labyrinthian caves of consciousness
At sublevels of awareness.

Here where they have sought reality,
Here where they have thought reality to be,
They have encountered and put on
An existence that is of the night.
And so coordinates of consciousness
Found in the substrata of being
Have provided no clue, no sign,
Except the clue of nonexistence,
Except the sign of death.
And so the existence of the not-self
Is a nonexistence—
Desires leading unto death
And death unto desire.
And the cycles of karma roll,
And mankind in twilight consciousness
Impose the rule of sin and struggle
Where purity and victory might appear.

I come to clear the mental densities
And to carve a pathway
From subterranean chambers
Unto the Himalayan heights.
I penetrate the depths of astral consciousness
Where Mara has enslaved humanity.[2]
I come with a light,
A threefold light of faith and hope and charity.
I come forth from nirvana the Enlightened One
Carrying the torch of the ages.
Let the souls who would be free,
Who would search and find the way,
Follow me in this hour of the Glorious Day.
And so as the Mother descends into the earth
To claim her own,
I come also to claim the light of God-identity.

I AM the Buddha.
I come quietly.
And to all I now proclaim:
There is an escape from darkness unto light.
There is a way wherein the soul takes flight.
I point the way.
I AM the way.
I AM the Buddha of the light.

Now learn of me.
My way is clear.
At Shamballa threefold-tier [3]
Foundation of the law
Of wisdom's power and love's own bower,
Tripartite light connecting hearts the world around
With heart of God,
Reveals the sacred mystery of my way.
For in the balance of the graces three,
There is the consuming
Of all hatred, lust, infatuation.
There is the extinguishing
Of the law of self-perpetuation.
As the candle of the not-self
Is snuffed out in an era of time and space,
So, too, the errors of mortality
Are swallowed up in God—immortality,
The singularity of the One.

And from the ashes of the former self
The threefold flame ignites
Nobility, honor, and love.
These three reveal the way of wisdom
And of wisdom's throne.
So let those who would attain the path
For every error now atone.

Let all proclaim the victory of the light
And in his law delight.
Let all proclaim my way,
The way of peace
And of freedom in love's release.
Let all know this hour
That nirvana, as the consciousness of God,
Is attainable here and now—
When to selflessness you vow
To seek the way of bliss,
The reunion of happiness,
When by your faith,
Your hope, your charity,
The soul's approbation
Echoes in the temple of being:

There is a way.
I AM the way.
There is an escape from human consciousness.
I AM the way.
I shall find the way.
I shall search until I have become the way.
And when I have found
Surcease from this mortal round,
I shall not take the leap,
The giant leap into the arms of God,
Until I have cleared the way
And beckoned to humanity
And set forth the law
By example without flaw.
And so the Buddha I would be,
And so the Buddha I would see.

The path of attainment in the Buddhic light
Is to pursue the way of perfection
And, when the perfected way is found,
To leave the reward of highest goal
And to return to time and space
And the evolutions of the race
To hold the torch,
To lead captivity captive
To the law of selfhood lived in God,
To anoint the blinded eyes with the spittle
Until they see men as trees walking,
And then the Buddha talking,
And then the Christ upon the mount,
Until the blinded know their blindness
And are blind no more,
Until the stubborn, willful,
Kick no more against the pricks
Of their own karmic recompense,
But embrace the Saviour on the way,
Experience that blindness for a day.

This not the blindness of the cave,
But the blindness of the light
And of the brave
Who dare remove themselves from Mara's toils
And starve the senses for awhile,
Until these false defenses
Of the nonexistence of the not-self
Are replaced by the senses of the soul
And the soul expanding like the sun—
Whirling, fiery center—
Enters a solar consciousness
And knows God as the cosmic void.

This is nirvana:
The place where God is real,
The store of energy whereby you heal
The wounds and the war scars
Of these little ones.
And so I say to all today
Who choose to walk my way,
Who choose the Buddhic ray:
Be prepared to take the torch of life,
But not unto thyself.
The torch is for humanity,
And it is carried
Only by those who have extinguished
The candle of the lesser self.
Now let us see
Who will follow the Buddha
On the path of hierarchy.

In the center of the flame I AM

*Gautama*

# 3. The Perfection of Alms

# Chelas Defining
# the Law of Perfection:

Indeed the story of Sumedha
Can be the story of your soul,
Of one who recognized the goal of Buddhahood,
Pursued it valiantly, and won.
The beginning of striving to be Buddha
Is self-mastery formulated from the fiery core,
The light that lighteth every man and woman
Born of the essence of God-Good.
Those who apply themselves diligently
To the law of the Christed ones
Are not afraid to make a strenuous effort—
As Christ did in Gethsemane,
Sweating "as it were great drops of blood"—
To vanquish the human will
And to declare "Peace, be still!"
To the tempest of human emotions
And the turbulence of the human intellect.

In order to be aware of Buddhic consciousness,
To even contain within soul and being
A recognition of the Buddhic initiation
And the ancient lineage of the many Buddhas
Who have come forth out of hierarchy,
Out of the Great Central Sun,
To manifest for humanity
The consciousness of the One,
You must have already prepared yourself
In the Way of the Cross and the fourteen stations[1]
Which define the victory of the Christ
In each of the seven rays.[2]

And thus Sumedha earned the right
To recognize the Buddha;
For the senses and the pretenses of the human
Had been set aside
And the apertures of the soul—
As chakras, faculties, and sensitivities—
Had been sharpened, quickened,
Filled with light to master the law of the seven rays,
To be the Christed one,
Anointed through self-discipline
And perseverance through adversity.
This is the foundation
Whereby the Christed ones prepare
To meet the Buddha on the way.
Therefore, attain God-mastery
In the law of the seven rays.
Therefore, come to Shamballa as victors bold,
As masters of the flame.
And by the humility you have attained,
You will recognize the conqueror on the way,
The Lord of All the World.

Because Sumedha—
Your own soul and mine—
Had determined to find the path
And to let nothing hold him back,
His heart was filled with joy
When he heard
That the Buddha called Dīpaṁkara
Was coming by the way.

While Sumedha was clearing the path
For the holy one of holies,
He meditated on the name of Buddha,
And within his soul he did proclaim,
"The Buddha comes!
All hail, the Buddha comes to reign!"
And as he was meditating
Upon the law of the three and three,
The six powers of the star of God-mastery,
And visualizing the image of the Buddha
Enthroned within his heart,
Lo, came the Buddha, came Dīpaṁkara!

The path was not yet cleared,
And so quickly he laid himself
Face down upon the mud
That the Buddha and his disciples
Might walk over him.
As Sumedha—
Your own soul and mine—
Lay waiting for the procession of the Buddha,
His contemplation was upon
The transmutation of corruption
That he might know and one day become
The Incorruptible One.
And he pondered in his heart
The securing of wisdom and all knowledge
Through Buddhahood.

With each such yearning of the soul,
With each such desiring to be whole,
The one in whom the flame of compassion burns
Now earns the right
To be the soul representative
Of the soul of humanity.

For he desires to achieve omniscience
Neither for personal adulation in this world
Nor for personal gain in worlds to come,
But to attain the Buddhic enlightenment
That he might be a Buddha here and now,
A Buddha for humanity,
A wayshower pointing the way
From this shore to the next.

Thus the desiring to be the Buddha
Must contain within itself
That humility which does provide
Totality of being,
That all mankind might walk
Over the body of the Buddha,
Might pass through his mind,
Might be nourished by his energy,
His self-mastery.
All this the soul lying face down in the mud,
The soul determined
On the path of selflessness in service,
Declares unto itself it must accomplish
Before taking leave of Terra
And entering into nirvana.

So then, Dīpaṁkara the Buddha
Approached Sumedha prostrate in the mud
And, stopping there,
Proclaimed to all the company that he,
In vast cycles yet to be,
Would be crowned a Buddha,
Lord of All the World.
The destiny not only of Sumedha
But of every living soul
Was proclaimed that day.

But the difference between Sumedha
And all other living souls that day
Was that he accepted his God-ordained destiny,
His responsibility to be the Buddha.
The soul that accepts future attainment
And the presaging of that attainment
In the ever-present now
Is the soul who seizes
The fiat of the Lord of the World
"Thou shalt be the Buddha!"
With the vow
"I AM the Buddha here and now!"

No matter how far seeming
From present awareness
Is the soul's own attainment of Buddhahood,
The soul must understand
That time and space afford opportunity to expand,
To prepare the self line by line,
And to put on the virtues
Of the wheel of perfection.
These virtues are flames of the one great flame,
Petals of the thousand-petaled lotus.
Therefore, instead of waiting
For a Buddha or a Christed one
To gain mastery of the soul,
The soul who determines to be the Buddha
Pursues with diligence
The ten perfections of the wheel of the law.
And as the cycles turn,
The foundations of Buddhahood are formed;
And one day the soul finds itself
A veritable magnet of the Central Sun,
Magnetizing the Buddhic light
Until it does become the Buddha all in one.

The first perfection of the wheel, then,
For all who with Sumedha would be the Buddha,
Is the Perfection of Alms.
It is the total giving of oneself,
The continual emptying of the jar of water,
That the jar might be filled again.
It is the self-emptying,
The bestowing of the energy of God freely.
This virtue is the testing
Of the measure of selflessness,
For only in the flame of selflessness
Are there found souls who can be trusted
With the energies of God's power.

Only in selflessness
Can the soul be trusted with omnipotence.
When the Lord God knows by the proof of action
That the soul can let go and bestow upon humanity
Every blessing that it has received from on high,
Then he will bequeath to that soul
Limitless energy and the powers
Not only of this world but of many worlds.
To learn to give is to learn also to receive
And to trust the law
That every thing that thou givest
And every good thing that thou doest
Shall return to thee tenfold
By the wheel of the law of the ten perfections.
This is a law which must be trusted
Before it can be tested,
And even in the testing it must be trusted.

The Perfection of Alms as a virtue fourfold
Must be perfected in the four lower bodies
By the application of the threefold flame.
Intelligence must govern giving,
And wise application of the law,
And compassion without flaw.
The Perfection of Alms
Is not casting one's pearls before swine;
Nor is it the unwise use of energies and talents
Entrusted to the care of the spiritual overseers,
The stewards of the race.
For every morsel of energy that is given
Must be well placed,
Secured within the heart chakra
Of both the giver and the receiver,
Then multiplied in grace.
By contemplation and meditation
Upon the Christ within yourself—
The subject of your giving—
Upon the Great Giver of every perfect gift,
And upon the Christ
Within the receiver of your gift—
The object of your giving—
You must come to know
That all givingness is to vest the self as God
With self-mastery in the law
And then to bestow
The love of Christ
Upon humanity here below.

This balanced flow of power, wisdom, love
Must needs be multiplied
By mastery of the sacred elements
In the body of the Mother.
Therefore, in the planes of Matter,
See how the tripartite flame of Shamballa
Will give to you the mastery
Of the Conqueror of the World
Over fire, air, water, earth.
Then see how
Etheric, mental, emotional, and physical
Vehicles of consciousness,
As spirals of the sacred elements of being,
Converge at the nexus of the mind of Buddha,
Receiving from God, giving to humanity,
Always abounding
In the joy of eternal abundance,
Precipitating omnipotence,
Omniscience, omnipresence.

And so for many lifetimes
Sumedha pursued the perfecting of this perfection
Until he reached the quintessence of the law
And gave not only his all,
But all of himself,
Offering up his own life that others might live,
Giving his own flesh that another might eat of it.

We remember the Christed one who said,
"Except ye eat the flesh of the Son of man
And drink his blood,
Ye have no life in you."
Therefore the ultimate in the giving of the self
Is when the soul realizes
That it must give itself as light,
As the Christos,
As spirals of Alpha and Omega,
To be assimilated by the body of mankind.
In this giving,
The candle of the lesser self is extinguished
And the threefold light of real identity is ignited.
This is the first step to nirvana.

I leave you with the contemplation
Of the first of the ten perfections.
When your contemplation
Becomes unmitigated action,
The Lord of the World will proclaim you
The master of the Perfection of Alms
And you will have begun
The path of the Buddha.

I AM waiting to receive you
Into the thousand-petaled lotus of my crown.

*Buddha*

# 4. The Perfection of the Precepts

# Chelas Resolute
# in the Mastery
# of the Ten Perfections:


And so the Lord Dīpaṁkara
Prophesied the future
Of the future Buddha.
Behold the disciple of the Lord!
Behold the devotee of the Word!
Behold the one! Lo, he has come!
Sumedha in the world to be,
A Buddha in the world shall be.

He spoke of his great retirement
And of his struggle fierce.
He spoke of his austerities—
The conqueror Dīpaṁkara—
Of his sacrifices
And of the compassion
Of that one, Sumedha,
Who would be known
As the Compassionate One.

And to all the multitudes
The Lord did proclaim
The future name of this beloved son,
Of his mother and his father,
Māyā and Suddhodana,
And the name bequeathed to him
From ages past, from cycles vast—
A name emitting
From a causal body of the sun.

And from out that sun,
The I AM THAT I AM,
Would be born the soul
Of the Sakya clan.
Gautama his I AM name translated
For the Buddha that would be,
For the Buddha yet to see
The fire of God
Descending like a rod—
A flaming spirit out of heaven
Come to earth to be the leaven.
Gautama is his I AM name,
Gautama the name of sacred flame.

Dīpaṃkara spoke
To all the people gathered there
Of events foretold
And the law of old
Written in the Book of Life
Whereby the sons of prophets and of kings
Would come forth
In future time and space
Recycling energies of karma and of dharma[1]
And the distillations of the law,
And the poetry of the songs of angel devas.
So this son of sons,
This king of kings,
This Buddha of the Buddhas
Would come forth
To meditate beneath the ajapāla tree
And, tarrying there,
Receive the rice pottage
From the maiden fair.

Then to seek and find
The stream Nerañjarā,
To bathe therein,
To put on the adornment of the saints,
To form the pellets forty-nine
Of the rice pottage all refined,
Then to go the way,
The conqueror's way,
To the place of the tree of wisdom.

And Sumedha—
A soul fearless in the right,
A soul brilliant in the light,
The one of glory
Descending from the throne of grace—
Would take his place
Where every Buddha
From the beginning to the ending
Had sat,
From Alpha to Omega wending
Over spirals of cosmic destiny—
The place for entering the heaven world,
The place on earth
Consecrated by the Lord of Lords.
Under the fig tree he would sit
In the place immutable,
Of the law irrevocable.
Here wisdom's fount and wisdom's throne
Adorned by Buddhas of the ages.
Here one day would Sumedha come
To face the East from the immortal bo tree.

Here resolute in wisdom absolute,
One day in cycles yet to come
This devotee,
Lying here before you
Face down upon the mud,
Will come to face
The cosmic consciousness of the One
And enlightenment endure.
Behold the Buddha of the future!

As in the drama of the Christed ones
And avatars of the ages
Their disciples were foreordained,
So, too, the disciples of Gautama
Were named by Dīpaṁkara.
As all who would participate
In the five-pointed star of mastery,
Of Cosmos' secret rays,[2]
Must pursue the mastery of the ten—
Five points without, five points within—
So the future servitors of Gautama
Must the initiations of the five,
The secret rays, invoke.

As keepers of the flame,
Moggallāna and Sāriputta,
Tempering the mighty flow
Of wisdom here below,
Must hold the threads of Cosmos' consciousness
And of the *antahkarana* of a cosmos[3]
As that cosmos
On the warp and woof of the Creative Mind
Should pass through
The heart, the soul, the mind—
The chakras of a Buddha yet to be.

And Ānanda must hold forth
The third of the secret rays
As point of transition
For the two chief disciples of the masculine ray
And the two chief disciples of the feminine ray,
Khemā and Uppalavannā.
Then within the fiery core of the five-pointed star
Enthroned upon the throne of grace,
Gautama will take his place,
Holding the inner keys of the sacred mysteries,
Holding the law, the alchemy,
The wisdom, the compassion,
And the victory for all humanity.

When thus Dīpaṁkara had spoken
To mortals and immortals,
When he had prophesied the prophecy
Of the Buddha yet to be,
He and his procession moved onward,
Ever onward and upward in the law
And on the path of the Lord of All the World,
While Sumedha, soul of souls,
Archetype of humanity, patterned Buddha,
Archetype of the stars,
Arose from the way where prostrate he lay,
To rejoice and to reflect,
To prepare and to protect
The light of the Buddha yet to be.

And then pursued he diligently
The Ten Perfections of the Law,
And from out the ten thousand worlds of hierarchy
Came the proclamations
Of the masters of the Ten Perfections.

And they themselves attested
To the presages that are foreordained—
Events and cosmic happenings,
The melting of the elements,
The mastery of the wind and water,
And the quaking and the shaking
Of worlds within and worlds beyond.
All these and many more were witnessed
By the masters of the ten thousand worlds
Who did profess,
"Of a certainty and of a truth,
A Buddha of the future thou art."

Thus all the signs of the coming of the Buddha
Were fulfilled;
For the soul of Sumedha had God-willed
A destiny foreordained,
The destiny of a Buddha yet to be.
The soul of souls, the Buddha of Buddhas,
Would pursue with diligence
The quickening and the chastening,
The Self-elevation, the self-immolation.
And because Sumedha
Received the torch of the Buddha that day
And accepted the torch of Dīpaṁkara's ray,
In future aeons yet unborn
One called Gautama
Would hold the mastery sevenfold
Of the Seven Holy Kumaras,
The Lords of Flame from Venus
Who would unfold
The epitome of the law,
The sacred fire,
And the rekindling of threefold flame,
Of heart chakra, of Shamballa.

Behold Gautama, Lord of All the World!
Behold Gautama,
Holding the banner of Sanat Kumara!
Behold the Buddha of a soul!

The second perfection
Is the Perfection of the Precepts.
To practice and pursue the precepts of the law,
Sumedha flowed with the determination
Of the Mother of the World
To drink from the fount of her holy wisdom,
To assimilate each precept line by line,
Facet by facet, catching sparkles
Of the diamond-shining mind of God,
And, by the alchemy of the Perfection of Alms
Already perfected,
To make each facet of the mind of God
A sharpened arrow of the mind of man,
An arrow that would reach the mark in kind
Of the Creator's mind from whence it came.
Each arrow thus sharpened
A means of penetrating the impenetrable,
Until the thread of consciousness—
Threading the arrow
As though threading the eye of a needle—
Should reach the center of that Creative Mind
And there in love nirvana find.

There is a story in Buddhic lore
About the yak cow and her flowing tail
And the determination of that yak cow
Who will stand if needs be unto the death,
If perchance that flowing tail be caught
In brambles or bushes by the way.
For the yak cow will not allow
Her flowing tail to be tattered or torn.

More precious than life itself
To the yak cow is her tail.
So then, this is the teaching
Of the Buddha of Buddhas:
To guard and keep the precepts whole and holy,
To guard them still if the Buddha thou dost will,
To guard them forevermore
As the yak cow guards her tail.

And is not the tail of the yak cow symbolically
The extension of the energies of the Mūlādhāra?[4]
And these energies, do they not flow
From the fount of wisdom
Of the Mother of the World?
Is this not the Goddess Kundalini
And the fire of attainment
Whereby every Buddha does attain
To the enlightenment of the crown,
Ascending the scale of being,
The ladder of initiation from Omega unto Alpha?

So then, the one who would walk
The way of the Buddha
Must the perfections of the law perfect.
These ten for the mastery
Of the secret rays within, without;
And each of the five rays of the fiery core
Contains within itself
The mastery of the Father,
The mastery of the Mother.

From Alpha to Omega, from Omega to Alpha,
The soul that is resolute
In the mastery of the Ten Perfections
Ennobles the Soul of God
And the souls of humanity
With this discipline of the disciplines
Which comprise the wheel of the law.
And thus the Perfection of Alms
Is God-mastery in the masculine ray
And the Perfection of the Precepts
Is God-mastery in the feminine ray.
And these two comprise the test
Of Alpha and Omega
In the first of the secret rays.

During many existences Sumedha endeavored
To fulfill the precepts of the law.
The defining and the refining
Of these principles of power,
Of the omnipotence of the Lord of Lords,
Of the God of Very Gods,
He found within the fiery core of being
As the geometry of the One.
Thus defining and refining the law of love,
He acquired the Perfection of the Precepts
Until he became known
As the Keeper of the Precepts.
For the Law of the One,
For the Principle of Precepts,
He again laid down his life.

First he was assailed
As the vessel of cosmic consciousness,
As the divine memory of the gods.
This was the test of fire and of the etheric body.

And to attain where he had lain
Face down upon the mud,
The brave Sumedha, soul of very souls,
Surrendered that vessel of cosmic consciousness
Even then as he lay upon the sod.
And by the alchemy of air
And the wind of the Holy Spirit,
He proved the precepts in the vessel of the mind;
And the mental body was refined.
Line by line,
Moment by moment, minute by minute,
Sumedha passed the prerequisites
Of the sacred precepts.
He proved the mind of God
To be the mind of Buddha,
To be the mind of a soul all in one.
And in the raging of the fallen ones
And of Mara and his armies,
He proved the precepts as the molecules of water,
As the mastery of the water,
And as the sounding of the sea
And the pounding of the sea
Upon the rock of Christ,
Upon the mountain of the Mother,
Upon the diamond shores of the Logos.

But when it came to the mastery of the earth
And the alchemy of crystallization
And of the salt and of the pillars of the salt,
The body of Sumedha,
As Christ upon the cross,
Was pierced through and through
While the soul of Sumedha remained steadfast
In sublime contemplation
Of the God of Very Gods.

He kept the precepts to perfection,
Returning love for each affliction
Of the hordes of night,
Returning wisdom and the justice of God being
For each reaction to the Shining One,
The gift of God from out the Central Sun.
Their senses were defenses
Against the Buddhic light.
The flaming one remained a flame,
And they who sought to kill the body
Could not kill the flame.
And thus in the ultimate sacrifice,
Sumedha anchored for eternity
The golden flame of Buddhic light,
The golden flame of the precepts of the law.

That blessed one upon that blessed day
Knew well what others failed to know.
And so he confirmed the law
"This body that my soul does wear,
'Tis good, 'tis good—
Expendable for the cause of Buddhahood.
'Tis better, then, that I renounce
That which will be taken still
Ere the seasons turn
And the Eternal claims what is not mine to claim.
'Tis better that I exchange
The corruptible for the incorruptible
And give to God and man
What is only mine to give."

Thus given the choice
Between the immortal flame
And the mortal frame,
Sumedha chose to seal the flame
For humanity for eternity
And to commend to God the vanity,
The frailty of all mortality.

This is a choice
That every soul can make
In the here and in the now
And by transmutation's flame
Exchange the old man for the new,
Bring the Christ flame to perfection's view.
For every soul can choose
To perpetuate the vow
To the perfections ten,
Dying to the old ways,
Living to the new
According to the precepts of the law.
To every soul resolute in the mastery
Of the Ten Perfections of the Law,
I say pursue the precepts,
Pursue them without flaw.

I AM

*Gautama*

in the flawlessness
of the Buddhic flame

# 5. The Perfection of Renunciation

# Chelas Seeking
# the Third Perfection
# of the Law:

The conditions and the conditioning
Of a Buddha to be
Comprise a ceremony of cosmic majesty.
Not only the Ten Perfections and their definition,
But to define each perfection
From deep within the soul
Even before there is a teacher to point the goal—
This is the challenge of a Buddha yet to be.

Therefore, O soul of my souls, humanity
Moving toward the central star of divinity,
Carve out the Ten Perfections one by one
As a sculptor sculpts the face of God in stone.

This is not blasphemy. It is to atone
For every error of mankind,
To seek his rod and, in truth, to find
Line by line the measure of the law,
Line by line the face of God
Appearing in transcendent awe.
Therefore, O sculptor of the soul,
Take the blessed elements
Of air and fire and water,
And blend them into earth.
Carve there a soul of sacred worth.

And now let the soul,
The potential of the Buddha,
Be molded by the Potter.
Let it be filled with breath of Life.
Let the creation strike forth
The note of the Creator.

Souls merging in the flame of Buddhic mastery,
Now tell me I say,
Tell me the perfection of the three.
And as the perfection is reflected in the perfector,
So tell me now, what is that vow?
Can you define the third perfection of the law?
For it is written, "Seek, and ye shall find." [1]

Now then, take a moment and meditate
Upon the fiery core of being,
And see what the Lord thy God
Doth require of thee.
And lo, Sumedha, your very soul and mine,
Called forth from God the third perfection
And perceived the image of renunciation
And all the saints and seers
In their service and surrender.
He saw them all and one by one
How they attained in wisdom
And in the second of the secret rays [2]
By renouncing all form and formlessness,
Even of the possessor and the possessed.

He saw the vision of the saints and seers of the ages
One by one renouncing time and space
And all and every thing under the sun.
He saw them coming line by line,
And then he meditated
Upon the contents of their mind.
And penetrating deep within the mind,
He perceived the reason of the Logos
And on this one perfection enlightenment attained.

The key to mastery, lo, I have found:
To view every mode and modification
Of this mortal round
As a prison house of the soul,
To understand the soul
Confined to Mater, time and space,
As the prisoner of the rock—
In misery and in suffering,
Confined and confining.
So each saint and seer,
Subjectively conceiving of the Self
A prisoner of the laws of mortality,
Having only one all-consuming longing—
That, to be free—
Regards the forming
And the unforming of existence
As a prison house of clay.
Thus in pursuing renunciation as the aim I AM,
Look to God and to the sun within.
Renounce all else and thus thy victory win.

And so the soul of Sumedha
And of the chela of the light
Wove a pattern through numberless rounds
Of existence within the carnal bounds
Until that soul, the one for the many,
Completed the perfection of self-abnegation.
By surrendering the all,
He attained the All.
And meeting Mara on the way
As Christ, too, was led up of the devil,
So the kingdoms of this world he renounced,
And turned away from worldly honor
And worldly acclaim,
And in renouncing the kingdom
And the desire thereof,
Gained the kingdom within
And the kingdom above.

The kingdom—
It is consciousness of life's immortal bliss.
The kingdom—
It is self-knowledge of a higher ego
Than the world can know.
The kingdom is the containment
Of all forces in heaven and on earth.
It is God-control of every facet of the soul.
With the true kingdom of consciousness
Comes a greater defining of identity,
A greater sense of selfhood,
The strength of the Divine Self,
And the crowning by the Lord God
Of the one who has shown the right to rule
Not as heaven's fool
Nor as the folly of the earth,
But in wise dominion
And the dome of wisdom's worth.

He that would be great among you,
Let him be the servant of all.
He that is great among you
Is the servant neither of self
Nor of passion's pall,
Not of desire save the desire to be
The Buddha for humanity,
Not of attachment
Save the attachment to the law of individuality,
Not of self-centeredness
Save the centering of the self in God—
This the way of renunciation,
This the way the soul of Sumedha trod.

And now there are footprints
In the sands of the Gobi Desert,
Once a Gobi Sea.
There is a path to Shamballa clearly marked.
Do you see?
Now let your heart burst forth
In poetry and song.
Now breathe a prayer
That every soul be free from wrong—
Free to pursue the path of right,
The Eightfold Path,
To the center of God-delight.

Here on the altar of Shamballa,
Enter now the threefold flame,
The flame of Christ-renunciation,
The flame that is the fifteenth station
After the way and the cross
And the fourteen aspects of the seven rays.
Come, come to white-fire core
And that fire ablaze
With pink and blue and golden hue
And rainbow radiance of the Creative Mind.
Here in Shamballa come and find,
Come and find me in the center of the flame
Where all who renounce
The modes of time and space
Live in eternity to reign.

I AM in the lotus of Shamballa,
The Shamballa of your heart's desiring to be free.

## *Gautama*

of the light

# 6. The Perfection of Wisdom

# Chelas Searching, Searching for the Ten Perfections:

"Seek, and ye shall find!"
Is the fiat of the Creative Mind.
Seek and ye shall find,
O my soul, Sumedha,
Dwelling in the soul of humanity.
Sumedha, awaken to thy God-reality!

When I had the third perfection of the ten
As renunciation found,
I longed for completion
And fulfillment in this round
Of mastery of the second of the secret rays
To coalesce the second point
Of the five-pointed star of self-awareness.

Therefore to wisdom's crown
I gave the all of my devotion—
To the crown of a Buddha yet to be,
The crown which one day
The Lord would place upon me
If I the Ten Perfections sought
And the battle of the serpent fought.

The meeting of the serpent mind
And the defeating of that mind
By the action of the law of God—
This is the testing of the mettle of a soul,
The fourth perfection of the golden scroll,
Sifting, sifting grains of energy,
Separating by weight and measure and facet
Each nugget of gold, each diamond shining
In the crystal stream of energy flowing,
Flowing from the fount of reality.

To seize from God at his behest—
And only by his command—
The sacred fiery rod,
The scepter of authority,
And then to go forth
To pounce upon the serpent in his lair
And to plunge the rod of wisdom
Through and through—
This is to slay the dragon at its inception,
To replace it with the Christ-conception.
To destroy the seed of Mara
That the seed of a Buddha might spring forth—
This is the test and the testing
Of the fourth perfection of the law.
To expose the lie behind the serpent
Coiled inside the bag,
To free the devotee and the Brahman
From every woe and mortal foe—
This is the bravery of the soul.

Determined in the Perfection of Wisdom,
The soul, as precipitation
In the Matter of the Mother,
Can now come forth.
No longer shall the dragon stand
Between Omega and her God;
No more can carnal consciousness divide
The lotus from the crown.
Now on earth as in heaven,
The fusion of caduceus fires
Flows freely as the River of Life:
Father-Mother God, one in manifestation,
Prove the wisdom of the law of Christed one,
The soul anointed to be Buddha in the way.

And so, my soul, expose the lie!
Expose the lie as energy coiled and entwined
Like an overgrown bramble vine
Choking off the life-force of humanity.
And so, my soul, in wisdom know
The Goddess Kundalini;
Invoke the upward spiraling energies
Of Mother Divinity.
And by these let the brambles and the briars
And all serpentine mires
Fall lifeless to the ground
To be consumed in the fires
Of the purity of the Mother.

Now, soul of souls,
To gain the wisdom of the Mother,
Seek the sacred energy
And determine to have no other.
Then thread by thread,
Intone the wisdom of the law.
Weave the seamless garment without flaw.
And as the crowning glory
Of the crown of crowns,
Embroider the lace of bridal veil—
A veil of purity to consume the veil of maya.
Seek wisdom as a holy oil,
As the blessing of the marriage
Of the soul to God.
Wisdom's oil anointing thy crown
Will release the fragrance
Of the thousand-petaled lotus
When the soul of a Buddha
Becomes the Buddha
In the power of the three-times-three.

Now these four perfections of the law
Are for the mastery
Of the disciples of the Buddha
In the perfection of the points
Of the first and the second of the secret rays.
As one by one you take your parts
Among the company of the saints,
Let your mandala be
For the fulfillment of God-mastery
As all the sons and daughters of light
Give their sacred energies
To the Perfection of Alms, of the Precepts,
Of Renunciation, and of Wisdom.

And now let souls come forth
Who would carry the flame of Ānanda,
Chosen one carrying the fires of transition
And the waters of derision
Whereby the gods do mock
The armies of the evil one
While holding forth, as keepers of the law,
The torch for those who now cross
The ever-flowing stream of time and space
To enter the sacred place
Where virgin consciousness doth atone
For the sin of all mankind
Unwittingly committed
Against the Mother of the World.
Now let the banner of the Buddha be unfurled
As Ānanda comes forth to teach
The way of the fifth perfection and the sixth—
The way of courage and of patience,
The only way whereby the Alpha
Becomes the Omega
And the fusion of the Father-Mother God
Gives birth to the Christ
In the chosen disciple of the Lord of the World.

I am Gautama.
I come to rule.
I am the Buddha
Born within the heart of humanity,
Carrying souls striving for the Buddhic light
To the place where God dwells
In Himalayan heights.
There I am enshrining the crown of the Buddha
As the crown of life for all
Who will master the Ten Perfections.
Will you mount the path
And claim my every footstep as your own—
And then the pinnacle of perfection in the law,
The crown of five stars
Waiting at the summit?


I AM

*Gautama*

in the silence of the highest peak
of the highest mountain of the world

# 7. The Perfection of Courage

# To All Who Would Walk
# in the Way of Courage:

Courage is the sign
Of the coming of age of the heart.
The heart that knows no fear—
For love is there—
Is the heart that is mature,
Where perfect love, love perfected in the law,
Has cast out every fear and the torment thereof.
As the lion roars in the jungle,
The king of the beasts,
So let the sound of the chela
Be the roaring of the heart,
As the fires of creation
Burning in the bowl upon the altar
Proclaim the Christ
King of Kings and Lord of Lords.

Courage is for the mastery of the third secret ray,
And this ray is the excellence
Of the divine alchemy of self-awareness.
It is a ray that requires
The God-control of the Christed one of Aries
Multiplied by the power of ten.
Thus courage and patience go hand in hand
As the spirals of Alpha and Omega
To complete the action of the secret ray
That is midpoint between the first and second
And the fourth and fifth.

And so, my friends,
Friends of Sumedha
And of the souls of humanity,
Let us study together that which makes courage,
That which makes patience,
That you might safely master the secret rays
And find the reward
Of going within to the white-fire core,
The end of all your labors.

Courage is watchfulness.
It is the heart that is full
Of the awareness of the All—
The heart that by intuition is aware
Of every infringement upon the All,
Every infraction upon the Whole.
Those who keep the watch
As watchmen on the wall of life
Must have the courage to defend
The citadel of consciousness
And the secret chamber of the heart.
And the watchman who walks
Upon the wall of the Lord
Must be prepared for every foe
And every form of consciousness
That would leap as a beast in the night
Out of the depths of the jungle,
Out of the astral plane,
Where the emissaries of Mara wait
To taunt and to tempt the guardian of the heart.

To be the watchman is to be the lonely one,
To be the keeper
Of the gate of Christed consciousness
And of souls aborning in time and space—
Souls tender, innocent, and helpless
In the womb of the Mother.
And so as knight champions of old
Who came to guard the fold
And to seek the chalice of the Lord,
Come one, come all
Who the Buddha would be.
Come to defend the age of God-mastery.

Courage is the flame of endurance—
Enduring through the night,
Overcoming the greatest of all foes that is fear.
And the ally of fear that is doubt,
And the culminations of spirals
Of fear and doubt
Which are set forth as the laws of mortality.
These dragons of the deep
Come forth disguised as ghosts of the mist.
They masquerade in all their masks
Of human questioning and querying,
All for one end, and that end alone
To take from the watchman
The countenance of courage
And the roar of the son of God,
To deprive him of the victory of self
Before the dawn when, with the early light,
Angels of the Christ come to ordain
The morning of the Mother.

And so you see,
It has ever been since the fall of the fallen ones
That denizens of darkness
Have moved against the souls of child-man
With fear and trembling
In the hours of darkness
And the hours of the moon
To take from tender souls the gift of the dawn
That is the love of the Mother,
Her comfort and her presence,
Reborn day by day
As promise of fulfillment in love's own way
On love's own ray.

Therefore let the answer come forth
From the watchman on the wall.
When the cry is heard,
"Watchman, what of the night?"
Let the answer be:
"All is well! All is well!
For God is whole and I am whole.
And in that law of harmony,
I take the rod of power,
The scepter of authority,
And I mark upon the sand
The circle of our oneness.
And I declare, They shall not pass.
They shall not enter here.
Nay, they shall not defile
The virgin consciousness.
I am the watchman on the wall of life."

Now you see,
Keepers of the Flame of Life,
Of the Buddha for humanity,
The enemy is ever ready
To send forth waves of fear
Even while you are winning,
Even as the light crests unto the victory.
For when all else is lost,
The enemy will inundate the souls of light
With tidal waves of fear.
It has well been said,
We have nothing to fear but fear itself.
Just as the sense of struggle makes the struggle,
So the enemy seeks to win in the battle of life
By convincing you through fear that all is lost.

Take heart I say!
Come of age within the threefold flame.
Claim the I AM name
As the light of Shamballa,
The heart of Buddha where you are.
Shamballa, the heart of a planet,
Bursts forth the fire of courage.
So be the heart of life where you are,
The heart of a family,
Of loved ones and friends,
The heart of a community,
The heart of a nation.
And let the sound of the heart
Be the roaring of the lion.

Then know, too, that your own beloved Mark,[1]
Who mothers the arc of consciousness here below,
Takes also as his signet the lion of Saint Mark.
The lion is the sign of the attainment of the heart
And the one who carries the flame with courage,
Saying to all who walk along a pilgrim's way:
"Fear not, for I am with thee.
Take courage. Be of good cheer,
For I am the flame of love
And wisdom and power ever near."

Let the mark of courage, then,
Be energy released with alacrity,
With fastidiousness to detail,
With a keen sense of timing
And an utter awareness of space
Hallowed by the presence of the Holy Ghost.
Let courage be determined action,
A will fired by love,
Seasoned by wisdom,
Matured by the flow of integration
In the Mother's love.
By the flame of courage
That is closely allied with the cosmic honor flame,
The greatest victories of all time have been won.
And by the absence of courage,
Where fear has seized and gripped
The hearts of humanity,
The greatest defeats of all time
Are recorded in the annals of cosmic history.

Courage is the mark of those who will to win
And those who have won again and again
Each battle of Armageddon
Over thousands of years
Of the defense of the Mother flame.
On every front, in every city
Where souls of light
Merge their flames for the victory,
There the eagles gather as the forces of light
Drawn by the corpus Christi of the Lord.
There, too, the dragons come
With their fire and smoke,
Breathing upon the light-bearers of the age.

On guard! Draw your swords of living flame!
Stand, face, and conquer!
And let the rapier thrust of the sacred Word
Be the fire that proceeds
Out of the mouth of the two witnesses,
The fire of the word that devours the enemy.
Therefore invoke the fire of the throat chakra
Of the messengers of the Lord,
And see how the Lord God in this age
Will turn back the enemies of the New Jerusalem.
See how the Lord God of Hosts
Will defend his people
Even as he defended the children of Israel
And prepared the way unto the Promised Land.
Take courage, take courage, O hearts of fire!
Proclaim your victory!
Proclaim the light of God that never fails.
Stand before the tribunal of the world
And speak the truth,
And see how the truth will make you free.

I rejoice to behold
The envelopment of your being
In the cosmic honor flame,
In a sheath of white fire that is the courage
Of the Elohim and cosmic beings.
For once you taste the sweet elixir of victory
And you know the laurel wreath
Of the conquering hero,
You will understand
That when you have displayed courage
Through the unity of the Christ consciousness,
One with God is the majority
Of the victory in any battle,
On any front, anywhere in cosmos.
And when you have seen the results of courage,
Determination, forbearance,
And a steady moving tempo
Marching into the light of the sun,
God in you and your own soul, like Sumedha,
Will never ever be defeated again.

Forevermore may your heart be sealed
In the flame of courage.
Forevermore may you dissolve
All errors of the past,
All failures of the past,
All specters of the night
In the dazzling golden white light
Of the courage of the heart—
A heart fired in adversity,
A heart sealed in the diamond of God's love.

To the victors of courage
Belong the spoils of the human consciousness.
The spoils
Are all of mankind's misqualified energies
That spiral into the flame of purity.
And in that conflagration, that transmutation,
There is returned to the victor
Sacred energy of life
Purified for the overcoming of all strife.
To the victor also
Belong the fruits of overcoming
Of all the saints and ascended beings.
To the victor they gladly give
Of the momentum of their causal bodies.
Thus in the nexus of the heart of courage
There flow the energies of humanity
Purified in the crystal stream of God-clarity,
And in that heart
There flows an abundant measure
Of the I AM THAT I AM.
Thus Christ the victor, Jesus the noble son,
Sealed in the heart of courage, did proclaim,
"All power is given unto me
In heaven and in earth."

Therefore, O my soul—
Soul of Sumedha, soul of humanity,
Soul of chelas on the path of the Buddha—
Clear the heart, the sacred chamber.
Expand it wide and long.
Increase the height, the breadth, the depth.
And when the way is all made clear,
Welcome the mastery of Dīpaṁkara here.
Welcome the Buddha, the Lord of Lords,
The conqueror on the way.
Welcome the Lord of All the World
Into your heart,
Into the flaming flame of sacred fire,
Of honor, courage, and purity.
And see how God will dwell
Within the chamber of your heart.
See how the fire will swell.
See how the white light will swirl
To the movement of the pulse of Shamballa.
See how the expansion of consciousness
Will come to those who have the courage to be.

I AM the Buddha in the heart of humanity.
Summon now your divinity.


*Gautama*

# 8. The Perfection of Patience

# To All Who Would Enter
# into the Communion
# of the Saints:

Just as courage is the sign
Of the coming of age of the heart,
So patience is the sign
Of the coming of age of the soul.
And patience is the understanding of the saints.
It is the long-suffering of those who above all
Would harmonize the light of the soul
With the flow of cosmic law.
For this is the patience of the saints—
To endure all things
Until the fulfillment of the law of cycles.

Those who would return
To the white-fire core of being
Via the sorrowful way
And the way of the mastery
Of the five secret rays
Must come into alignment
With the inner blueprint of life
Through trial and tribulation
And through the testing of the soul
In measures of discipline
That are for the trying of the patience of the saints.

There will be times—
Mark my words well,
Chelas of the Buddhic light—
When you will be required to stand fast
Against the hurricane of the astral plane.
And you will stand upon the rock of Christ
And cling to the Tree of Life
As the fierce wind and the storm,
Violent in its vituperation,
Becomes the unleashing of the black magic
Of Mara and his band
Against the soul who dares to stand
In the place where the Buddha has stood
To proclaim the law.

In that hour of trial, remember the bo tree,
And let your refuge and your strength
Come from God on high,
Who has set his seal upon you
To be the Buddha of the law.
Every erg of energy that seems to be the adversary
Must be counted as karma
And as the dharma of the soul.
Consider then the law of cause and effect.
Consider that you yourself have sown the wind
And that if you would enter
Into the fiery core of being,
You must first reap the whirlwind.

So then, in order to pass the test of the ten
And of the five secret rays,
You must know that you are God—
God in actuality, God in manifestation,
God in every aspect of your expression.
More than knowing,
You must be the Creator in the creation.
You must render unto him
The things which belong to him.
Every organ in your body
Is a focal point for the release of God's light.
Every cell and every system
In the physical temple
Is designed to be the instrument
For the flow of God's energy
Into the physical octave.

You must know that God lives in your heart
As the threefold flame of Shamballa's light.
You must know
That God is the seed identity of your soul.
You must know
That God is a sun blazing in every chakra.
But more than that,
You must understand
That even the physical organs
Are instruments of the Lord's expression.

When you declare, "I AM THAT I AM,"
You must not exclude the temple.
Therefore, let God be your brain
As well as your mind.
Let him be your physical heart
As well as the spiritual chamber therein.
Let him be your eyes, your nose, your mouth.
Let God be your lungs and your liver,
Your kidneys and your gallbladder, if you will,
And every good thing which he has made
As an instrument for the flow of the law.

Think not this a desecration.
For I tell you that if you would be
The body of God upon earth,
You must seal
Every part of that body in light daily.
And when you call forth
The protection of Archangel Michael,[1]
You must see the physical
As well as the spiritual complement
Of the whole being
Charged with blue-white lightning
Flushing out the toxins that are physical
And the poisons that seep from the astral plane
And attach themselves to molecules of light,
Causing disintegration, old age, disease, and death.

When I went forth from my father's house
And saw for the first time
The factors of mortality—
The plight of decrepitude, a diseased body,
The lingering of death,
And how these three
Imprison the flame of being,
I felt the power of God
Welling up from within my soul,
And I heard the fiat of my own master
Declaring the truth of being:

I AM the life everlasting
I AM the life universal and triumphant
I AM the life overcoming sin, disease, and death
I AM the glory of the law
And the glory of the victory
I AM the Word incarnate
Make me free, make me free,
Make me free, O Siddhartha!

I heard the call,
I heard the compelling of the Logos,
And the fire burned
Within my heart and soul and mind.
I saw the mists of maya,
I saw the temptations of Mara,
And I knew that I must take my stand
Unflinchingly, unceasingly, determinedly.
For mankind must be free
From the stain of sin
And the sordid aspects of selfishness.
Mankind must know the law.

In order for mankind to know that law,
I must be that law through and through.
I must not exclude the body,
For the body is the Mother.
I must not allow the forces of disintegration
To attach themselves to my body temple
Or to any part thereof.
I must wield the sword of the Mother
To defend truth
In every atom and molecule of Matter.

By thus proving that God himself
Can and shall dwell in the tabernacle of Matter,
I would prove for all eternity,
For all evolutions descending into this vale of tears,
That there is a way out.
And that way begins with the flushing-out
Of all debris and discord
Of the human consciousness.
And that flushing-out can be brought about
Only by invocation to the flame;
For only the flame of God blazing,
Blazing in every plane of cosmic consciousness,
Has the power to consume all wrong
And every desecration of the Divine Mother.

I AM the Buddha of the law.
I am patiently waiting for mankind
To come into the awareness of responsibility and,
With that, the responsibility
For bearing one another's burden,
For carrying a balanced burden
On both shoulders—
To the right the weight of personal karma,
To the left the weight of planetary karma.
Thus I wait for mankind to possess their souls
In the patience of the fulfillment of the law.

This is the great call of the Buddhas of the ages—
The call to come into the communion of the saints,
To wash your garments
In the crystal flowing stream
Of the Mother chakra,
To dip into the Ganges,
And to know that God can purify,
God can sanctify,
God can make holy
Even the muddied waters
Of the great River of Life.
And so God,
In the patience of the fulfillment of the law,
Can also sanctify the bread and the wine
As the flow of the blood of Christ
And of the body of the Lord.

Chelas of the Buddha,
Look up and live in the light!
For miracles are happening every day.
Remember the miracle
Of finding a four-leaf clover.
Remember the joy of searching, searching,
And then picking that four-leaf clover
And knowing that the law of God in nature
Was proof that life is good.

The miracle of the three-leaf clover
Is the miracle of the threefold flame,
Of the sacred trinity
Of Brahma, Vishnu, and Shiva,
Which Saint Patrick taught
To the good people of Ireland
As the trinity of Father, Son, and Holy Ghost.
Now understand
That when you have found the four-leaf clover,
You have found the Mother.
And the fourth leaf is for the crystallization
Of the God flame in Mater.
It is for the amplification of the light.
It is the purity of the Mother
That releases the power of the Father,
The wisdom of the Son,
And the love of the Spirit Most Holy.

This is the miracle of life—
That the saints in their patience
Await the coming of the Mother
Into manifestation,
That the saints endure the return of karma,
Of every astrological aspect, of every effect
Which they have set in motion as cause.
And the saints receive into their four lower bodies
Personal and planetary karma,
And they draw into the fiery vortex of the heart
All energies requiring transmutation—
Enduring, enduring all that the law requires
For the fulfillment of the promise
Of the coming of the Mother.

Run to greet her on the path of life!
Strew the flowers gathered in the fields.
Strew them along the way.
Let little children, with their chubby hands,
Pick the flowers for the coming of the Mother.
Run to greet her!
For with every step
Upon the ladder of Buddhic initiation,
You approach the fiery center,
The womb of the Starry Mother.

She comes along the path.
See her in the distance descending the mountain,
Over the hills and into the valleys—
She comes to gather her children.
She comes to receive them, one and all,
Into her arms of love.
Without discrimination the Mother comes.
She sees no flaw at all among her children.
Each child to her is a precious flower
Of the heart of the Father.
And her love for the Father
Is such that her adoration unto him
Makes of every child born of his heart
A flower in her bouquet of praise.

When you greet the Mother,
Give to her the flowers you have picked;
For she will take them
Gladly and joyously to her heart,
There to place them
Upon the altar of the Christ,
A gift of the children unto the Father.
In the name of love, then,
The Mother is the mediator of the flow
From the Father unto the children
And from the children unto the Father.
She is the intercessor of his great wisdom
And of their incomparable innocence.

To have and to hold the gift of the Mother
Is worth the exercise of patience.
Therefore, patiently, patiently
Invoke the transmutation
Of all that the law doth require of thee.
Patiently search for the four-leaf clover.
Patiently pick the wild flowers in the fields of life.
And receive both the tempest and the calm
As the sign of the coming of the Lord
And the turning of the wheel of the law—
Receiving, receiving the fruits of all planes
Into the fire of the heart
For the glorious consummation
Of Alpha and Omega.

I AM in the patience of the law
The Buddha forever.

*Gautama*

# 9. The Buddha and the Mother

# To All Who Would Be
# United in the Love
# of the Buddha
# and the Mother:

Courage and patience
Are the twin flames of Alpha and Omega
In the white-fire core of the third of the secret rays.
Understand, then,
That courage is the thrust of Alpha
That sweeps the planet round
With the intensity of the will of God
In the power of the spoken Word
And as the beacon of the all-seeing eye
Rotating from the window of the lighthouse,
Pointing the way of victory
To the souls of humanity
On the path of Buddhic initiation.

Courage is the crown of the Absolute
And the measure of the wisdom of the soul
Wherein courage becomes
The patience of the Mother—
Patience as the God-control
Of energies in motion,
Patience as the sun
Shining in her strength in the solar plexus,
Rays of Starry Virgin
Shining upon the just and the unjust.

Courage is the wisdom of the soul,
The quiet knowing
That all mankind shall be made whole
In the immaculate conception
Of the patience of the Mother,
Whose perfect work shall manifest
The day of the Manchild's appearing.

The Mother is calm
Because she is the master
Of the science of the immaculate conception.
By her immaculate vision
She guards the consciousness
And the seed atom of Alpha and Omega.
She guards the blueprint and the fiery matrix
Of child-man aborning in time and space.
And in the guarding of the all-seeing eye
And the vision of perfection for every child,
The Mother holds the reins
Of power, wisdom, and love.
Within her patient heart you hear the strains
Of cosmic melody,
Spirals of energy precipitating man and woman
Made in the image and likeness
Of the I AM Presence.

Patience is the virtue
Whereby the saints do magnify the Lord
And the feminine ray
Becomes the handmaid of the law.
Patience is the flow of purity
Waiting for each initiation,
Keeping the vigil of the wise virgins,
Keeping the light of the chakras
For the reunion of the twin flames
Of Alpha and Omega.

And so my soul, Sumedha,
Heard the call of courage and answered,
Acquiring the fifth perfection of the law
Through the mastery of water
And energies in motion
In the sea and in the sea of the astral plane.

As Jesus stilled the tempest
With his "Peace, be still!"
And cured the disciples of their dreadful fright,
So in the midst of a stormy sea
Where all were affrighted unto the death,
I entered the inner mind of God
And found the key to the perfection of courage.
As Saint Germain,[1]
When he crossed the ocean wide,
Was upheld by the goal
And the promise of a new world
When all around him
Entered into the mutiny of their fear's rebellion,
So the soul of Sumedha
Pressed on in the dead of night,
Mastering the raging seas
By the promise of attainment
In the light of the Buddha
In a world to be.

Likewise, souls mastering the perfections
In the twentieth century
Must here and now come to grips
With the dark threatenings,
The tempestuousness of life's storms;
For these consist of the return of mankind's karma
And their misuse of the energies
Of the Mother flow.

And thus the world in these times
Is being inundated
By the records of the Dead Sea
And the blackness
Of their own misqualified energy.

Let the chelas of the Buddha
And those who have claimed
The way of Sumedha as their own
Now summon the ray of Alpha
And Alpha's thrust,
Now summon the ray of the Mother
And the Mother's trust
To hurl the light into the depths,
To reverse the tide of darkness
Into the white-fire core
Of the flame of transmutation,
And to bear with equanimity
The thrashings and the lashings
Of those who are the instruments
Of your initiation
In the sixth perfection of the law.

To endure suffering when endurance is required
Is a virtue,
But you must adjudicate the cycles.
You must know that when courage is satisfied,
Patience will follow with her perfect work;
And when the work of patience is perfected,
It is time for courage
To displace the darkness of that space.

Therefore, endure all
That the Great Law doth require of thee
And demand answer from the Buddha of the law
For the energy of courage to consume by fire
That suffering which is superfluous
To the attainment
Of the Ten Perfections of the Law.

Understand, too,
That the gift of the wisdom of the law
And the instruction which you receive herewith
From my own heart flame
Is the comfort of the Spirit
In the days of tribulation
When the saints are required to endure all things.
For he that endureth unto the end of cycles,
The same shall be saved
From the toils of the wicked,
From the temptations of Mara,
And from the negative spirals
Of his own returning karma.

In love is the gift of patience.
For only love
"Beareth all things, believeth all things,
Hopeth all things, endureth all things." [2]
Indeed, the man who in love
Endureth temptation and persecution
For his right use of the law,
When he is weighed
In the great balance of the Buddha,
Shall receive the crown of life
Which the Lord Buddha has promised
To all who love the light in the law of being.

I dwell upon this initiation
Of the third of the secret rays
That you might understand
That it is for the entwining of the flame
Of the Buddha and the Mother
Within your own fiery core.
Cells of being marching in pairs
Emulate the twin flames of Alpha and Omega.
And when, therefore,
You find no other explanation,
No other consolation
For the sorrow and the suffering
That for a little while
Precedes the rejoicing and the overcoming,
Look to God on high,
Look to the Lord Dīpaṁkara
And the disciple Sumedha.
Look to the soul within
And hear the voice of hierarchies
Echoing from the central sun of life:

"I AM the Lord thy God
Visiting the temple of being,
Testing the mettle of the soul, and releasing—
Unto that soul who has called forth
The light of opportunity—
Verily, verily, the opportunity to enter into unity,
The unity of the One,
By retracing those cycles
Which although nobly begun
Have ensued in failure and frustration
For want of consecration
And for want of putting down
The temptation of self-preservation.

"Extinguish that candle of the lesser self
Ere it does scorch the garment
Of the Christed one to be,
Of the Buddha on the path of golden immortality.
Extinguish the candle of the lesser self.
Leave it not to burn on in the night,
For it will scorch
The blessed filigreed veil of Cosmic Virgin.

"I come with energies of Kali
To flail the arrogance of the dying ego,
Of the beast that riseth up out of the sea
And of the beast that cometh up out of the earth.
For these would destroy thy sacred alchemy,
The alchemy of the union of the soul with God.
This is the goal of life reigning in sun and sod.
In the detail of the law,
Discipline thy vanity, O chela!
Become Sumedha, soul of souls,
O sacred worth of light in humanity!"

Let the shavings
From the soap carving of a little child—
His carving of the image of the Buddha—
Demonstrate to parents and to teachers
Who would instruct these little ones in the law
That if you would prove to souls
The light of God without flaw,
You must shave away the propensity,
The density, the superfluity of vanity of vanities
And that personality cult
Based on the interchange
Of senseless conversation,
Sensual vibration, ego argumentation,
And the development of the human personality
At the expense of the divine.

Look not for human personality
In the chelas of the Mother,
But for charisma of soul
And the quietness of the Buddha.
For they who follow
The Eightfold Path of sacred worth
Know the Buddha within the heart
And the quietude of communion
In the heart of God,
The heart of Christ, the heart of humanity.
And so in patience possess the soul.
Be the possessor of the lines of force;
Be the controller of the flow of energy.
Let the light of the Creator
Manifest in the fourfold aspects of thy being
As the four lower bodies of four-leaf clover
Show the precipitation
Of the Mother and the Buddha.

Patience is the holding-on to the reins
Of the all-power of God in heaven and in earth.
Patience is tenacity,
The clenching of the teeth for the victory,
And the willingness to wait—and to wait
Through the cycles of the night and the day
For the coming of the Mother ray
And the coming of the Buddha and the law.

You do not know the hour
Of the coming of the Son of God
Into your heart,
Nor do you know the hour
Of the coming of the Lord of the World.
Therefore, in the patience of the saints,
In the courage of the righteous,
In the wisdom of the masters,
Tarry ye till I come.
Tarry in the City Foursquare,
Tarry in the New Jerusalem,
Tarry in the bowl of the chakras.
And while you tarry,
Let the outgoing of your energy flow
Be the thrust of Alpha
And the receiving of the oncoming light
As the wave that crystallizes
The foam of the Mother's love.

I AM the Buddha
In adoration of the Mother flame within you.
Raise up now that Mother flame,
That I might behold the object of my adoring.


*Gautama Buddha*

# 10. The Perfection of Truth

## Chelas Becoming the Life
## Universal and Triumphant:

Truth is the seventh perfection of the law.
Truth is the crystal flowing stream
Of consciousness without flaw.
It is truth that frees mankind
From the bane of error.
And what of the vanity of vanities?
Truth is willingness to assess actualities—
To stand, face, and conquer
What is manifesting here in time and space.
To stand at the nexus of the cross of being
And to admit to oneself the right and the wrong
Of thought and feeling, word and action—
This is to be a pillar of truth.

Let us not prevaricate; let us not equivocate.
Let us place our case squarely
On the foundation of truth.
Truth is an invincible shield,
A mighty armor of the Lord
And of the law of the Lord
Shining in his righteousness.

Truth is the sword of the sacred Word.
Truth is the understanding
Of absolute perfection in the I AM Presence
And of absolute compassion in the Christ Self.
Truth is the understanding
Of the soul and of many souls
Striving to become one with the Absolute.
To claim the truth of the immaculate conception
Is your right and your duty;
But to reverse the roles of the Christ and of Mara,
Of the Real Self and the carnal mind—
This is to imprison the lightning of his splendor.

Now let Wisdom teach her children
The precepts of the law.
To retain the energy of the Holy Spirit
Without flaw
Is to perfect the crystal chalice of self-awareness
That it might contain the flow
Of Mother's energy sparkling in the sun,
Bursting through the crystal matrix of her love.
Chelas of the Mother
Have been taught to define selfhood—
On one hand to set forth
The truth of the attributes of reality
Which exist as the blueprint of identity
At the fiery core of being,
And on the other hand to draw the lines
Of obvious karma and the manifestation
Of the consequences of sins
Of omission and of commission.

If you have a bad temper,
Do not deny it before God,
Before self, or before your peers.
But have the courage,
Which you have won
As the fifth perfection of the law,
To confess your fault.
Be humble and be patient
To ask thy companions on the Path
To keep the flame for thee,
To tarry and to pray for thee,
To uphold thy bodies and thy soul
Through the temptations of the night.
Call for the reinforcements, the guardian angels;
For all the hosts of heaven and of earth will serve
The soul who is willing to acknowledge
The absence of the Divine Whole in manifestation.
Blessed are they who know
They are poor in Spirit;
For in acknowledging their impoverished state,
They affirm the vacuum
That is then filled by the Spirit
And they gain thereby the kingdom of heaven.

What shall be, then, your affirmation of truth?
What shall be your denial of error?
Claim the calm God-control,
The equanimity of consciousness and of flow
Which you know your Christ Self to be,
Your God Self to be.
Then command the atoms and molecules
Of lesser consciousness
Into the flame of living truth
As you pray unto the Lord:
"O God, I believe! Help thou mine unbelief.

O God, the I AM in me is the perfection
Of my temper and my temperament.
Help thou mine imperfections.
This is my earnest confession before the Christ
Who stands at the altar of sacred being
In the temple of my heart."
Thus you invoke the purging fires
Of the Buddhic light
And you make progress,
Though sometimes painful,
On the path of truth.

Watch out! I say watch out
For the self-deceptions of the ego
That claims a separate existence from Reality.
Many among mankind
Have such a momentum of self-deception
That it is, as you say,
A defense mechanism of the unreal self.
And that self has convinced the soul
That in order to survive in the world,
It must continually compromise truth
Or rearrange the facts
So as to protect that self from harm.
But the greatest harm of all
Is the denial of the Real Self
That results from the practice of deception.
Therefore, keep a balanced course
As the morning star twinkling in the heavens
Makes the sign of the dove descending
And you hear within your heart
The approbation of the Lord
"This is my beloved Son—
This is my beloved Daughter—
In whom I AM well pleased."

Mark well the statements that you make.
Listen to your words.
Remove exaggeration, imagination,
Vain and proud talking
Calculated to impress another.
Beware recounting past sins
To impress fellow disciples.
Beware recounting those most sacred experiences
That must be held between guru and chela
Inviolate in the silence of the All-knowing.
Beware the taking of the joy of freedom's flame
And turning it to misqualification
In vulgar stories and base humor
That appeals to the carnal elements
Of the human consciousness.
Feed not the vile demons with vile speech,
And refrain from swearing.
As Christ said, "Swear not at all;
Neither by heaven; for it is God's throne:
Nor by the earth; for it is his footstool."
And let the statement of your reason for being
Echo the words of the avatar
"To this end was I born,
And for this cause came I into the world,
That I should bear witness unto the truth."

Plant the markers
Of the triangle of your consciousness
Firmly in the sands of time,
And let the coordinates of your space
Be poise and equanimity posited in Reality.
Withdraw the sting and the poison of the viper
By denying the power of error,
And confirm and bear witness to the truth
That "God is the all-power of being
And the only power that can act."

Understand that this statement itself
Is a consuming fire that will transmute
The cause and core of error's claim.
But recognize that
In the crucible of relativity *in tempus*
There is the finite existence of error
That must be challenged, that must be checked
By the thrust of the mind,
The proclamation of the law,
Invocation to the sacred fire,
And decrees offered unto the divinity of your soul.

It is not scientific
To face the chaos of the carnal mind
And to turn your back and say, "It is not real,"
*If* you do not understand that in transition,
In that band of consciousness
Through which you are evolving,
Man and woman whom God hath made
Have assigned by free will
A temporary reality and a temporary existence
To that error which is the fabrication
Of their own consciousness.
Man and woman created in the image of God
Are co-creators with life.
As co-creators having free will,
They have sent forth those imperfections,
Those laws of mortality,
By which they have bound and imprisoned
The energy of God.
Thus they have imprisoned the lightning.
Thus they must take the key of sacred alchemy
And unlock the prison doors
And set the captive free.

Thus in the name of the I AM THAT I AM,
The creative potential of a cosmos,
Man and woman must withdraw
All misqualified energy
From matrices of imperfection,
From patterns of error.
Man and woman on Terra have endowed evil,
As the energy veil, with life.
They have proclaimed maya as real,
And they worship
At the feet of the human personality
While failing to render just judgment
Of the actualities of the Now.

As Morya says, be willing to call a spade a spade,
To face the dark, the ugly,
And the sordid aspects of self.
For you have yet to slay
The dweller on the threshold,
The conglomerate of human creation
That will one day rise
From the depth of the subconsciousness
As "the beast that ascendeth
Out of the bottomless pit."[1]
And then you will be forced to behold
The accumulation of all that has conspired
Against the truth of being
With the consent of your free will.

Practice maketh perfect.
And in the proving of the law of being,
You must day by day wield the sword of truth
To slay the lesser dragons.
For the ultimate test will surely come,
And you will stand as David before the Goliath
Of your own erroneous consciousness.
There will be no one to blame
But your own lesser self
And its ratification of the law of mortality.
Nevertheless, if you follow the way
Of the Christ and the Buddha
While there is yet time and space,
You shall stand all one in the flame of living truth
That has become the majority of your being.
For you shall have focused reality by proof—
By proving each precept of the law.
And it will be the spiral of truth
That has become the sword of truth
Which you will use to pierce the heart
Of the beast of self-deception.

Now let each worded cadence,
Each phrase, each thought and feeling
Be measured against the absolute truth of being
And the actualities of the plane of relativity.
Now let assessments be made
Based on that which has in fact been externalized
As virtue or as vice.
And let us proceed
From present levels of attainment
To build our castles in the sky
And to secure the bastions of identity
In the foundations of that castle
Grounded on the rock of truth
Secure in the mastery of the Mater plane.

And when truth means more to you
Than life itself,
You will, with the soul of Sumedha,
Gladly give your life in sacrifice
To set the warriors of truth free.
Therefore, be willing to keep your word,
To keep the covenants of the promise
You have made to God and man
At the sacrifice of life or limb if necessary.
Above all,
Consider then the equation of truth whereby,
In the flow of the Word,
The comfort of the Holy Spirit becomes the truth
That is applicable in the moments of time
Descending in the hourglass of space.

Let truth be loyalty
To the cause of the Brotherhood.
Let it be the defense of the purity
And the integrity of the Whole.
Let truth be the protection of every earnest soul,
But let it not be a hiding place
For a den of thieves.

Truth will win
If you have the courage to proclaim it;
For with truth comes the judgment,
And with the judgment
The rendering of the measure of karma
To the left and to the right of the scales of being.
Truth is a catalyst for progress.
And if you must be stripped
Of your garments of outer consciousness
Until you stand naked before God and man,
Then let it be in commemoration
Of him who was despised and rejected of men,
Who stood in the place of the flame of reality
And was not afraid
Of the ultimate exposure of consciousness.
For he who abides in the flame of truth
Has nothing to hide.

Never mind, precious ones,
For the law will fulfill the exposure
With or without your consent.
As it is written: "There is nothing covered,
That shall not be revealed;
Neither hid, that shall not be known.
Therefore whatsoever ye have spoken in darkness
Shall be heard in the light;
And that which ye have spoken
In the ear in closets
Shall be proclaimed upon the housetops." [2]

Sooner or later the Great Law will proclaim
Every aspect of being that is less than truth.
Therefore, leap as a joyous emerald fire
To proclaim the truth,
To confess all that is undesirable!
And see how compassion,
As the flame of love,
Will exalt in you and fire in you true being.
See then how identity will increase
Spiral by spiral!
For you have dared to be the truth.

I am in the flame of God-reality
Witnessing unto the truth of the ages.


                        I AM

                    *Gautama*

                    of Shamballa

# 11. The Perfection of Resolution

# Chelas Striving to Enter
# into the Nobility
# of the Flame:

Those who would ensnare mankind
In the lies of the not-self
Have taken the great impersonal law of being,
The very truth of life itself,
And perverted that flame
Into the personality of evil.
They skillfully entrap mankind
Into identifying with the mass consciousness
And the veil of maya that enshrouds the planet
In a garb of mourning.
By and by, individuals allow
Their chakras to become funnels
For the flow of dirty energy that contaminates
The rivers and streams of consciousness
Which make up the network of the mass mind
And feeling body of a planetary evolution.

Now the individual takes in and takes on
The vibrations that sustain
The energy veil called evil
And personalizes,
Through impure action and vibration,
Whatever aspect of this force and forcefield
May be magnetized to his world
Through conscious and subconscious cycles
Of negative karma.

Therefore, you must understand
That as long as you disguise the errors of the past
In the modes of the human personality,
You yourself will always be guilty
Of personalizing evil.
And then there follows the syndrome
Of shame and remorse
For the evil that you have personalized
Through thought and feeling, word and action
At the very point of reality
Where in truth God is realizing himself
In time and space independent of mortal folly.
When the dawn cometh,
When the sun of being riseth
And you behold the Real Self
Free from the contamination of sin,
Then the white-fire core of being
Will soar as the dove of the flame of purity
To consume the cause and core
Of both personal and impersonal error.

Understand, precious ones,
That the sins which are common to the human race
Have been imposed upon mankind
By the fallen ones
Who have tattooed upon the subconsciousness
The lie that man and woman are inherently sinful.
As you approach, then, the altar of resolution,
The eighth perfection of the law,
Know that you must instill the clarity of truth
As awareness of selfhood
And deprive the fallen ones of their booty
By denying their claim to the personality of evil.
In the absolute awareness of being,
There is only the personality of good.
And this good is God in you the victor.

When you look upon the fallen ones
Who embodiment after embodiment
Have personified the energy veil,
You see in their faces the mark of nonexistence,
The grayness of the not-self,
And you see the whited sepulchers
Hollowed by inharmonious spirits
When they could have been hallowed
By the law of the one all-pervading Spirit.
Mark well my words:
When the unquenchable fire comes
In the baptism of the Holy Ghost,
The chaff, as the seed of the wicked generation,
Is burned up in an instant and is no more.

Be free from the lie
That evil is any part of your real personality,
The personality of your soul.
Recognize that this energy veil
Has been superimposed upon the law of being
Like a shroud, smothering the soul,
Preventing the flow of the breath of the Holy Spirit
That would daily cleanse
And purify and renew life.
Only when you take the sword of truth
And pierce the many masks
Of the human personality
Can you be rid of the contents of the mask—
That erroneous consciousness which cannot exist
Outside the mold of the human personality
With its claim to reality.

Now then, let us consider
The Perfection of Resolution.
This is the testing of the soul
In its invincible awareness of the Whole.
How can you be resolute
If you are not first founded on the rock of truth?
How can you be immovable
As the mountains of Lemuria,
As the Himalayas and the Rockies,
When you are uncertain of who you are,
What you are, where you are?

To be firm, to be established in the law of being,
You must know identity as the I AM THAT I AM
And you must proclaim yourself
A devotee of the Buddha and,
Like Sumedha, a Buddha in the world to be.
And those whose destiny it is
To carve in the clay of consciousness
The Madonna of the Lilies,
To be the Mother of the World,
The polarity of the Buddha,
Must also claim the I AM name
As the flame of the Mother.
To define the Real Self and then to expose
The usurpations of the office of the Real Self
By the carnal mind,
To dig them out fiercely—mercilessly—one by one,
And to refine step by step all that is contained
In the hallowed circle of being
That you call "myself"—
This is to make progress on the Path.

The Path is a spiral
Moving to the center of the white-fire core.
Many have not entered there
For many incarnations.
For while advancing on the track
Of the spiral that is the fire infolding itself,
They have come to a halt,
A narrow pass in rocky heights.
They have turned back.
They have said: "The air is too refined.
I cannot breathe the atmosphere of Spirit.
The climb is too rigorous and my pack too heavy.
I will tarry in this niche of consciousness
And make the trek to the summit another time."

The delusions of time and space
Have ever been the weapons of deception
Employed by the fallen one.
And his emissaries will always tell
The soul moving toward the center of being:
"Another day, another year
Is suitable for the surrender.
It is not necessary
To put yourself under undue pressure.
Remove yourself for a time
From those fanatical ones,
Those devotees of the flame.
Your path is not their path.
There are many paths.
Take it easy. Rest yourself along the way.
You have earned and you deserve
A much needed repose."

This is the line of the fallen ones.
And to it they add
Whatever line of reasoning appeals most
To the rebellion and the perverseness
Of the not-self.
They say: "Take time out from the Path
To indulge your family and your friends.
For if you do not, they will curse you;
They will leave you.
And then you will be alone,
And you know that you cannot make it alone."

What will you answer
When the lies of the wicked come like smoke
Seeping through the cracks in the window
And underneath the door?
If you inhale the stench of the Liar and the lie,
You will find yourself delaying the overcoming
Until you are overcome by the delay.
For delay is the attenuation of energies
That ought to be concentrated in the crucible.
But he who is the flame of living truth
Has proclaimed, "Behold, I come quickly!"[1]
The trial by fire
Must be administered by angels of fire
Who quickly scorch the human consciousness
As angels of the harvest
Burn the stubble of the field
To set the soul free from the debris of carnality
And clear the soil for a new sowing.

The swift and sudden coming
Of the lightning of the mind of God
Is the Lord's instrument
For those who would be victorious
In the way of the tempter.
For in the moment of victory,
An intensity of soul fire must be sustained.
And this sustaining of the fire
Is intended to remain so and not to be dispersed;
For once the fire is dispersed,
The ability to summon
The full measure of strength required
Is lost and you must await another cycle
For the concentration of energies.

The fallen ones know that the cycles of life
According to the law of the yang and the yin
Are alternately for the concentration of God-power
In the masculine ray of the Godhead
And then the release of that power
Throughout the Cosmic Egg in the feminine ray.
Victories are won
In the concentrated white-fire core
Of the masculine ray (the yang).
Then comes the ritual of the sustainment
Whereby the victory spans the cosmos
With the light of joy
As the burst of life from the heart
And the feminine realization (the yin)
That I AM God here and now and everywhere.

Beware the fables of the fallen ones.
For they will taunt you and try to take from you,
Surely as I am the Buddha of the World,
Your firm resolve to be unshaken
By the boisterous winds that sweep across the sea
To test the moorings of the tree
Planted on the hillside of the world.
Are the roots deep enough and firm enough
To hold the trunk and branches in their place?
Are you grounded in the law,
O my soul, Sumedha, soul of humanity?
Are your feet firmly planted
In the soil of the Mother?

Take care, O my soul,
To be resolute in the precepts pure.
Take care when the attractions
Personifying the animal magnetism
Of the lower nature
Draw thee to the dark pools
Of astral consciousness.
There is no other time
For the resolution of the victory than the now.
No other time or space exists
Except the here and now.
Past, present, and future
Are contained within the now.
The now is the moment of causation.
The now is the moment of self-realization.
And the here is the point
Of the precipitation of the God flame.

You cannot act in the past or in the future
Except you act in the now
To correct the wrongs of the past and to plow
A straight furrow for future beginnings
As well as the harvest of your winnings.
See then how Mara, that fallen one,
Has stolen from the Mother and her children
Pearls of opportunity for self-transformation.
Again and again he has taken portions
Of that which belongs to the Mother,
Segments of time and space,
In order to use the coordinates of relativity
Unto the destruction of souls.

Now, chelas of the law,
Seize from the fallen ones
Their domination of time and space!
Challenge the cycles of the energy veil
Which they have spun
Over the coordinates of time and space
Like a spider's web to catch the souls of light!
Take the sword of truth and of resolution strong
And sweep it through that spider's web,
And see revealed instead
Starry bodies
Adorning the firmament of God's being
Hanging in the skies.
Now, my soul,
Realize that these are the starry bodies
Of those who have seized
The coordinates of time and space
And used them to the glory of the Mother.
These are the starry crystal fragments
Of the Christos
Assuming their role in the mystical body
Of the Buddha and the Mother.

See how you can become where you are
A starry body instead of the procrastinator
Who defies the Great Initiator
By turning his back upon the tests,
Walking away from the flame
And into the hornet's nest.
When you leave the haven of hierarchy,
You will find the mob of the astral
Waiting to eat your flesh and drink your blood.
Like vultures and vampires of the night,
They pervert the sacred ritual of the Eucharist
Which the saints do share.
Therefore, affirm your resolution.
Be willing, then, to give your flesh as meat indeed,
Your blood as the elixir of life
To devotees who follow you
On the path of initiation under Maitreya.
For if you turn away from the light
And the true path of the Christ and the Buddha,
Surely it shall come to pass
That the fallen ones will consume
The being and the consciousness
Of the one who has an unclear,
Undefined awareness of selfhood.

You are not jellyfish!
You are not protoplasm suspended in the brine!
You have a starry blueprint
And a skeletal framework
Which the Lord God has framed and draped
With sacred essence of the body of the Mother.

Be swift, my soul!
Be swift to invite initiation—
To take it from the heart, the head,
The hand of the Mother.
And know that hierarchy is releasing to you
The confirmation of being
Through each successive step of initiation.

I am the resolution of the law within you.
I am the confirmation of true being.
I stand immovable upon the rock.
Stand with me, and we shall see
The stillness of the stars
After the hurricane has passed.

I AM at Shamballa the Buddha of the lighthouse.


*Gautama*

# 12. The Perfection of Goodwill

# Chelas Seeking and Finding
# the Ninth Perfection
# of the Law:

Now hear the word of the Buddha of the flame!
Hear the word that speaks
From out the flame within your heart!
Behold the rising spirals three,
Patterned course of solar destiny!
Behold the intertwining of Brahma, Vishnu, Shiva!
Behold the braid of fire
That crowns the head of Cosmic Virgin!

In the ninth perfection of the law,
Discover now the sacred formula
Of the Master Alchemist,
The mystery of the three-times-three.
Goodwill, it is the ninth perfection,
Three times three.
The flow of blue-fire energy
Is for the building of the pyramid of the soul.
Three times three, it is goodwill
That seals Creator and creation in the Whole.
Three times three, blue-fire energy
Of goodwill as fire flowing,
Sealing the matrix of your resolution
Of the precepts pure—as mental knowing
And crystal water cleansing, invigorating, glowing.
The power-wisdom-love of the three-times-three
In goodwill come full circle,
Flawless blue-white diamond
Hidden in the earth of the Mother.

Let goodwill flow to the right hand and to the left,
To friend and foe alike.
As the sun shines upon the just and the unjust,
So for the sake
Of soul expansion and soul freedom,
Be a solar disc
Shining through the crystal of the mind of God.
Be alive and brilliant
In the oneness of the three-times-three!
Dare to stand in the presence
Of the one who ensouls goodwill
As the law of cosmos!
Dare to make your aura the aura of the Logos!
Stand, O my soul, in the place
Where the sun of goodwill caresses the mind,
Refreshes the body,
And implants the kiss, a diamond dewdrop,
On the petal of the rose of the heart.

The action of the three-times-three
Is the balanced integration
Of the ascending triangle of Mater
And the descending triangle of Spirit.
The law of the balance is the key to this mystery.
Contemplate the balance, then,
Of the threefold flame, of the scales of Libra,
The balance of the flow of energy
In time and space,
In the hourglass, the figure eight,
And the Maltese cross.
Meditate on the balance
Of the inbreath and the outbreath,
On the receiving and the giving
Of solar fires and solar breath.

Behold the enlightenment of the law!
Tend the fires of goodwill
For self-proclaimed enemies,
For the idolaters of your person,
For those who come at eventide
To bask in the fires of your hearth,
To sup at your table,
And to hear the word of wisdom.
Watch the flow! Watch the flow!
And see how goodwill is the key
To the redemption of all energy
Imprisoned in the dungeon of former selves
That you have willed.

Now will another self!
Now create in the image of God!
Decipher the code of creation
As you watch intently the molecules of goodwill
Flowing through all form and substance,
Through the air and through the water,
In the earth and in the fire—
Translucent spheres like sparkling prana,
Thought forms of Gautama
Released from the mind of the Lord of the World.[1]
Watch the flow of energy throughout a cosmos
And the solar systems of the atoms!
Watch the movement of goodwill,
And learn now this perfection to instill
In every chakra, in every point of flow.

For as above, so below,
The lightning of the mind of God
Will flow and flow and flow
Through every soul dedicated to goodwill.
Boundless energy!
Boundless creativity!
Freedom to move and to be in love
The perfection that you are
Is unlocked by the key of goodwill.

Let love be in your heart a consuming fire,
Burning the hatred of the aggressor,
Of the professor who professes anti-God
And the philosophy of the Liar and the lie.
Let charity be the handmaid of goodwill.
Let it be the ruby ray that pierces,
Like a laser beam,
Those who take counsel
To put to death the Christ, the Anointed One,
Your own Real Self.
Let charity be a flame that turns back
The vengeance of the fallen ones
Who would exact retribution
From the Mother and her children
For the death of Lucifer [2]
And the children of the wicked one.
Let goodwill expand now;
I say, let it expand
As a fiery blue sphere growing—
Growing in the hearts of devotees
Of the Buddha and the Mother.

When I walk the earth
Strewing flowers along the pathways,
In the valleys and the mountains,
Anticipating the coming of the Mother,
I shall look for, and I shall expect to find,
Chelas glowing in the meditation
Of the blue sphere of goodwill,
Chelas glowing in the action of goodwill.
I look for the eyes that sparkle,
For hearts abounding in joyousness and love.
I look for smiling, upturned faces
Waiting on the Presence all the day.
I look for those who listen
With intent to hear the word of goodwill
And then run to do that word, to be that will,
To prove the law as love in action,
In service, and in service, and in service.

Keep on keeping on,
Lovers of the Buddha,
Children of the Mother!
Be dispensers of goodwill
And mark the place where God doth will
The fullness of himself
In form and formlessness,
In the sanctuary of being,
In the soul and in the mind,
In the threefold fire
Burning on the altar of the heart.
Be goodwill
And see how God will fulfill himself
In the diamond in the center of the flame.

Now this day let that flame
Consume all retribution and the desire therefor,
And let your desiring be
For victory, for victory!
Let your desiring be to know the law,
To meditate upon the law,
To extend the law
Through consciousness throughout the cosmos
And then to watch intently
As atoms of goodwill,
As components of God's being,
Outpicture the geometry of God-Goodwill
Through time and space
Because you keep the image of perfection
As the diamond without flaw.

I AM in the heart of the flame
The Buddha of goodwill.

*Gautama*

# 13. The Perfection of Indifference

# Chelas Fulfilling the Cycles
# of the Ten Perfections:

We approach the tenth perfection of the law
With reverence as one would come
Upon a flowing stream on the edge of the wood
Where the meadow begins to roll.
The stream is the quietness
Of the flow of the Mother
Anticipating the coming of the Buddha.

I AM the Buddha,
And I come to meditate
Beside the flowing stream of consciousness
Of souls determined to reside
In the movement of the Logos
Where the meadow of the Mother
Reaches the boundaries of the Spirit
And the flow of being marks
The levels of consciousness where I AM,
Of my origin in the fiery glacier,
The crystal snows, the summit of the Presence.

I AM the beginning of the flow
Descending from exalted heights,
The I AM THAT I AM.
I AM waters running, running, rushing,
Rushing to greet the meadow of the Mother.

From the mountains to the valleys,
I AM the soul descending
To claim my very own, my essence.
And I know that in cycles yet to come,
I shall be transformed
As water becomes air and air becomes fire
And the alchemy of the soul
Once cradled in the earth
Is born again in the crucible of fire.

Now see how the power
Of the three-times-three,
As the foundation of the trinity,
Awaits the tenth perfection of the law.
Multiply the first three perfections
By the second three.
Then take that product and multiply it again
By the final three,
And see the bursting of the mastery of the tenth.
Let the Perfection of Alms,
Of Precepts, and of Renunciation
Be fused into one balanced triangle
Of power-wisdom-love.
Let the three become one flame—
The whiteness of a shield
And of the sword of the Spirit
Glistening in the sun.
Let the Perfection of Wisdom,
Of Courage, and of Patience
Now become one single taper to light the candle
On the altar of the Buddha.
Let the Perfection of Truth,
Of Resolution, and of Goodwill
Be the solid foundation
Of the house of the Mother.

Now 1 times 2 is 2, and 2 times 3 is 6.
Six, then, is the number
Of the first three perfections of the law.
And 4 times 5 is 20, and 20 times 6 is 120.
Thus two 6s plus 0 reveal the number
Of the second three perfections of the law
To be 120.

Follow my numbers carefully
As I show you the key to the mystery
Of the three-times-three.
Seven times 8 is 56, and 56 times 9, 504.
Thus 504 is the number of the ultimate three.
Let us add the digits of our pyramid:
Six plus 1 plus 2 plus 0 equals 9.
Nine plus the power of the ten
(Symbolized in the zero)
Is the sign of the first and the second three.
Five plus 0 plus 4 equals 9
In the power of the ten
In the final three perfections of the law.

Six times 120 equals 720.
Again, 7 plus 2 plus 0 equals 9
In the power of the ten as the multiplication factor
Of the first two sets of three.
Now multiply 720 times 504 and see
The power of the three-times-three: 362,880.
Adding once again the digits,
Three plus 6 plus 2 plus 8 plus 8 plus 0
Gives 27 in the power of the ten.
Adding again this sum,
Two plus 7 plus 0 equals 9 in the power of the ten.
Nine is the magic number.

And when you resolve
To perfect these perfections of the law
By the power of the ten,
You will be the conquering one—
The Buddha in the world to be.

What is the tenth perfection of the law?
It is that which seals
The action of the three-times-three
And the nine-times-nine.
It is called Indifference.
It is the equanimity of being which comes
When the mathematics of the soul is fulfilled.
The soul that has mastered the nine perfections
Can be like Mother Earth,
Showing neither animosity nor amity
To any or to all—
The passive receiver of hot or cold or sweet or foul.
In the power of the three-times-three,
The flame of the Mother transmutes
The vices and the virtues of her children.
The flame of the Mother
Is the poise of the three-times-three,
The poise of Shamballa and threefold flame.

The tenth perfection of the law
Is the balance between desire and desirelessness.
It is the point of the fusion
Of the active and the passive.
And through it
The power of the three-times-three
Is multiplied by tens,
By hundreds, by thousands,
By millions, by billions, and beyond.

The Perfection of Indifference is the zeal
That determines the quantity of energy
Entrusted to your care.
The three-times-three will be the nine,
The ninety, the nine hundred, the nine thousand,
The nine million, or the nine billion
According to your ability
To show indifference alike
To mockery and to praise,
To pleasure and to pain, to poverty or riches,
Adulation or indignation.
This is the tenth perfection of the law—
Indifference to the gratitude
Or ingratitude of mortals,
Indifference to their cursings
Or the garlands of their approbation.

Now let the ego be exposed
As the impostor of the Buddha and the Christ,
The Mother and the Spirit!
Now let the ego stand in the arena of the mind,
Naked before the Ten Perfections of the Law!
Now let the faculties of virtue
Expose the usurper of the throne of grace!
Let the real conqueror move in
To slay the beast of the carnal mind,
Take the sword of the sacred Word,
And with supreme indifference
Slay the dweller on the threshold of being!

If you will pursue and practice diligently
The Ten Perfections of the Law,
You will gain the momentum
Of the nine-times-nine.

And after you have walked
Around the arena nine times nine,
You will fear not to enter there,
Even as the toreador challenges the bull
Of mortality, carnality—vanity of vanities.

Enter now the champion of the flame!
Enter now the one who has nothing to fear,
Nothing to claim (as his own)
    Or lose except to choose
The victory of the Buddha and the Mother.

See how the victor bold meets every cunning
In the cowardice of the Taurus creation,
Defending the light of the Buddha's station.
See how the toreador watches every move—
The master of emotion,
    The science of pulsation—
                    To prove
He is not distracted,
But with noble art distracts the enemy within.
Caught off guard,
    The bull lunges forward
        To destroy the Christed one,
The Buddha of the Sun!
But the mantle of the Lord of the World
    Is the shield and the goad
        And the cape of the toreador—
            The dividing of the road.
See how he swirls it deftly—
    A prophet in his own right,
        Like Elisha, who smote the waters
            By Elijah's might.

The bull is blind,
   Blinded by the passions
      Of his two-eyed vision.
With all the borrowed energy
   Vested in his animality,
      He cannot win against the soul
         Who has mastered the ten—
The Ten Perfections of the Law.
He is unprepared for the incision.
   The crowd is in derision.
      The sword of the living Word
         Pierces to the core the bull creation!
And lo, the champion,
   The master over all sensation,
      Stands now in the center
         Of the circle of the One!
He is the victor!
   He is ready for his incarnation
      As the Buddha in the world to be.

I AM Gautama
In the center of the Flaming One,
The thirteenth of the Buddhas
Of the Shining One.
When the twelve disciples
Standing as coordinates on the circle,
Coordinates of the Lord of All the World,
Have pursued, like Sumedha,
The Ten Perfections of the Law,
I will come again
To release the second tier of my instruction
In the law of the Buddha and the Mother.

I AM the Buddha.
I have come quietly.
I go quietly into the flame.

## *Gautama*

# The Ten Perfections of the Law

The following diagrams are offered to clarify
your meditation on the power of the three-times-three:

"Multiply the [product of the] first three perfections by
the [product of the] second three. Then take that product and
multiply it again by the [product of the] final three..."

First Three Perfections

    1. Alms
    2. Precepts
    3. Renunciation

Second Three Perfections

    4. Wisdom
    5. Courage
    6. Patience

Third Three Perfections

    7. Truth
    8. Resolution
    9. Goodwill

"Let the Perfection of Alms, of Precepts, and of
Renunciation be fused into one balanced triangle of power-
wisdom-love. Let the three become one flame—the white-
ness of a shield and of the sword of the Spirit glistening in
the sun."

$$1 \times 2 \times 3 = \boxed{6}$$

"Let the Perfection of Wisdom, of Courage, and of
Patience now become one single taper to light the candle
on the altar of the Buddha."

$$4 \times 5 \times 6 = \boxed{120}$$

"Let the Perfection of Truth, of Resolution, and of Goodwill be the solid foundation of the house of the Mother."

$$7 \times 8 \times 9 = \triangle{504}$$

"Let us add the digits of our pyramid:"

(Adding the digits of the first two pyramids gives the sign of the first and the second three perfections of the law—9 in the power of the ten.)

$$6 + 120 = 6 + 1 + 2 + 0 = 9 + 0$$
$$\longrightarrow 3 \times 3 \text{ in the power of the ten}$$

(Adding the digits of the third pyramid gives the sign of the final three perfections of the law—9 in the power of the ten.)

$$504 = 5 + 0 + 4 = 9 + 0$$
$$\longrightarrow 3 \times 3 \text{ in the power of the ten}$$
(thousands, millions, billions, etc.)

$$\triangle{6} \times \triangle{120} = \triangle{720}$$

$7 + 2 + 0 = 9 + 0 \longrightarrow 3 \times 3$ in the power of the ten

$$\triangle{720} \times \triangle{504} = 362{,}880$$

$3 + 6 + 2 + 8 + 8 + 0 = 27 + 0 = 2 + 7 + 0 = 9 + 0 \longrightarrow 3 \times 3$ in the power of the ten

# Addenda

## "Behold, I will send
## my messenger..."

In order that she might fulfill the high calling of the messenger of the ascended masters—the same God-free beings who delivered the word of the Lord to the prophets and teachers of Israel and to the avatars of East and West— Elizabeth Clare Prophet was initiated by Saint Germain, the hierarch of the Aquarian age, and by El Morya, Chief of the Darjeeling Council of the Great White Brotherhood. Together with her late husband, the Messenger Mark L. Prophet, who founded The Summit Lighthouse in Washington, D.C., in 1958, Elizabeth Clare Prophet was called to set forth the teachings of the Great White Brotherhood for the next two-thousand-year cycle.

These teachings have been released as the Everlasting Gospel in Book I of *Climb the Highest Mountain*, which contains practical and scientific explanations of the mysteries of the Self and the soul's mastery of the energies of the cosmos, and in *Pearls of Wisdom*, weekly letters from the ascended masters to their chelas, Keepers of the Flame Lessons, and the numerous books and tapes published by The Summit Lighthouse for Church Universal and Triumphant during the eighteen years of the Prophets' ministry.

Responding to the call of the Holy Spirit to bring the testimony of the Logos to the people, the messengers have held conferences and seminars throughout the United

States and abroad. In 1971 they founded Summit University to offer disciples of East and West the ongoing revelations of the Christ and the Buddha and techniques for self-mastery and self-realization through the I AM Presence. Seeing the great need for children of all ages to prepare for the Path that leads to the one Source, they also founded Montessori International, a private school (preschool through the twelfth grade) to provide the foundations of excellence in secular education as well as a true culture of the soul.

On February 26, 1973, Mark Prophet took his leave of this earth, ascending to the plane of the I AM Presence to carry on his work with the ascended masters and to make contact with their unascended chelas yet striving toward the goal of reunion with the Source. Just eight weeks before, he had stood in the Keepers of the Flame Motherhouse in Santa Barbara, California, when he took his final dictation from Gautama Buddha. During that dictation on New Year's Eve 1972, the Lord of the World passed to Elizabeth Prophet the torch of illumination for the age, "a torch charged with the vital fires from God's heavenly altar and the conveyance of a vast mission to illumine the world's children and produce the blessing of true culture to the age and unto all people everywhere."

And so the messengers, "the other two, the one on this side of the bank of the river and the other on that side of the bank of the river," remain the servants of the Lord and of his children in Spirit and in Matter "for a time, times and a half," as Daniel wrote, that "many shall be purified and made white, and tried" and that "the wise shall understand."

Elizabeth Clare Prophet, known today to the devotees of the teachings of the ascended masters as "Mother" because of her devotion to the flame of God as Mother, instructs and initiates students of cosmic law during twelve-week retreats sponsored by Jesus the Christ and Gautama the Buddha at Summit University. She also lectures and holds retreats throughout the world while continuing the important work of recording the teachings of the Great White Brotherhood and directing the multifaceted activities of Church Universal and Triumphant. The sacred responsibility of her mission, centered in the flame of God's will, is to teach, initiate, and succor the children of the Father-Mother God during this period of transition into the Aquarian age.

# Lord Michael

In the name of the beloved mighty victorious Presence of God, I AM in me, my very own beloved Holy Christ Self, Holy Christ Selves of all mankind, beloved Archangel Michael, beloved Lanello, the entire Spirit of the Great White Brotherhood and the World Mother, I decree:

1. Lord Michael, Lord Michael,
   I call unto thee:
   Wield thy sword of blue flame
   And now cut me free.

Refrain: Blaze God-power, protection
   Now into my world,
   Thy banner of faith
   Above me unfurl;
   Transcendent blue lightning
   Now flash through my soul,
   I AM by God's mercy
   Made radiant and whole!

2. Lord Michael, Lord Michael,
   I love thee, I do;
   With all thy great faith
   My being imbue.

3. Lord Michael, Lord Michael
   And legions of blue,
   Come seal me, now keep me
   Faithful and true.

Coda: I AM with thy blue flame
   Now full-charged and blest,
   I AM now in Michael's
   Blue-flame armor dressed! (3x)

And in full faith I consciously accept this manifest, manifest, manifest (3x) right here and now with full power, eternally sustained, all-powerfully active, ever expanding, and world enfolding until all are wholly ascended in the light and free! Beloved I AM, beloved I AM, beloved I AM!

These decrees were dictated by the hosts of the Lord to the Messenger Mark L. Prophet. We include them for your meditation and your mastery of the science of the spoken Word.

## O Mighty Threefold Flame of Life
### by Zarathustra

O mighty threefold flame of life,
Thou gift of God so pure,
Take my thoughts and energy
And make them all secure.

Under bond of brotherhood
And understanding fair,
Send thee forth unto my soul
The gift of holy prayer.

Communication's strands of love,
How they woo by heaven's law
A tender blessing for the good,
Releasing holy awe

That draws me near the throne of grace
To now behold thy sacred face
And without fear dispense aright
The passions of pure God-delight
Which set me free from all that's been
The sinful nature of all men.

Christ, raise me to self-mastery,
The living passion of the free.
Determination, now arise
And lift me ever to the skies!

I AM, I AM, I AM
Enfolding life and being all
With the God-command
"Amen!" that shatters human pall.

I AM, I AM, I AM
The free—no bondage holds me back;
I AM the fullness of love's law
Supplying every lack,
And consecration in full measure
Is my will and God's own pleasure.

Saint Germain and Jesus dear,
Hold my hand with Morya's here
And let the love of Mary then
Be the wings to raise all men.

Until they all unite in love
To serve that purpose from above
That comes to earth at any hour
Responding to the call of power;
Send thy shining wisdom then
That is God's love
Expanded for all men.

I thank thee and I accept this done right now with full power. I AM this done right now with full power. This is the full manifestation of the law of love that raises me to my eternal victory, now and forever!

## O Mighty Light
### by the Goddess of Light

I AM light within, without,
Expand, expand, and forever expand!
Field of consciousness within, without,
Absorb God's light and then command
Light of God to forever expand!

Fill the world, the land, the air,
The sea and sky and everywhere
With awareness for I AM there,
Sharing God and joyous prayer—
Beyond the earth in outer space
Expand the power of cosmic grace.

Our God is there and everywhere,
And where I AM, O thou art, too,
To increase awareness of thy truth
And show me in my I AM eye
The holy beauty of the sky.

(Continued)

I see thy light of diamond hue
Sparkling, shining, through and through
The pores of self in body large,
The macrocosmic universe.
I AM with thee, O God, I see
The light expand as path to thee.
The power flows, my being glows,
And Christ within, without me shows

I AM the way to peace and power;
Thy Spirit makes me one this hour.
O God, demand and now command
Thy Presence in our holy band
Of devotees of heaven's grace—
Show me, command me to take my place!
In freedom's band I'll ever stand,
By victory's power I wake this hour
To feel, to feel that flow of power.

Blaze right through me, light of God,
Spiral nebulae, suns of light!
Blaze right through me, truth of God—
Fill my mind with great delight!
I AM thy grace, manifest here,
Thy perfect love is shining clear.

Command thy selfhood to be mine,
Expand, expand in heaven's name!
Command my soul to be thy flame,
Expand, expand, O Love Divine!

And in full faith I consciously accept this manifest, manifest, manifest (3x) right here and now with full power, eternally sustained, all-powerfully active, ever expanding, and world enfolding until all are wholly ascended in the light and free! Beloved I AM, beloved I AM, beloved I AM!

# Sweet Surrender to Our Holy Vow
## by the Ascended Master El Morya

Meditation upon the God flame:

Our will to thee we sweetly surrender now,
Our will to God flame we ever bow,
Our will passing into thine
We sweetly vow.

Affirmation of the God flame merging with the heart flame:

No pain in eternal surrender,
Thy will, O God, be done.
From our hearts the veil now sunder,
Make our wills now one.

Beauty in thy purpose,
Joy within thy name,
Life's surrendered purpose
Breathes thy holy flame.

Grace within thee flowing
Into mortal knowing,
On our souls bestowing
Is immortal sowing.

Thy will be done, O God,
Within us every one.
Thy will be done, O God—
It is a living sun.

Bestow thy mantle on us,
Thy garment living flame.
Reveal creative essence,
Come thou once again.

Thy will is ever holy,
Thy will is ever fair.
This *is* my very purpose,
This *is* my living prayer:

Come, come, come, O will of God,
With dominion souls endow.
Come, come, come, O will of God,
Restore abundant living now.

And in full faith...

## O Saint Germain, Send Violet Flame

Beloved mighty victorious Presence of God, I AM in me, thou immortal unfed flame of Christ-love within my heart, Holy Christ Selves of all mankind, beloved Ascended Master Saint Germain, beloved Mother Mary and beloved Jesus the Christ, the beloved Maha Chohan, Archangel Zadkiel, Prince Oromasis, all great beings, powers, and activities of light serving the violet transmuting flame, beloved Lanello, the entire Spirit of the Great White Brotherhood and the World Mother:

In the name and by the power of the Presence of God which I AM and by the magnetic power of the sacred fire vested in me, I invoke the mighty presence and power of your full-gathered momentum of service to the light of God that never fails, and I command that it be directed throughout my entire consciousness, being, and world, through my affairs, the activities of The Summit Lighthouse, and all ascended-master activities, worlds without end. In thy name, O God, I decree:

1. O Saint Germain, send violet flame,
   Sweep it through my very core;
   Bless'd Zadkiel, Oromasis,
   Expand and intensify more and more.

Refrain: Right now blaze through and saturate,
   Right now expand and penetrate;
   Right now set free, God's mind to be,
   Right now and for eternity.

2. I AM in the flame and there I stand,
   I AM in the center of God's hand;
   I AM filled and thrilled by violet hue,
   I AM wholly flooded through and through.

3. I AM God's flame within my soul,
   I AM God's flashing beacon goal;
   I AM, I AM the sacred fire
   I feel the flow of joy inspire.

4. The consciousness of God in me
   Does raise me to the Christ I see.
   Descending now in violet flame,
   I see him come fore'er to reign.

5. O Jesus, send thy violet flame,
   Sanctify my very core;
   Blessed Mary, in God's name,
   Expand and intensify more and more.

6. O mighty I AM, send violet flame,
   Purify my very core;
   Maha Chohan, thou holy one,
   Expand, expand God's lovely sun.

Coda: He takes me by the hand to say,
   I love thy soul each blessed day;
   O rise with me into the air
   Where blossoms freedom from all care;
   As violet flame keeps blazing through,
   I know that I'll ascend with you.

And in full faith I consciously accept this manifest, manifest, manifest (3x) right here and now with full power, eternally sustained, all-powerfully active, ever expanding, and world enfolding until all are wholly ascended in the light and free! Beloved I AM, beloved I AM, beloved I AM!

# Notes

## CHAPTER 1

1. In India, a disciple of a religious teacher (<Hindi *celā* <Skt *ceṭa* slave). A term used generally to refer to a student of the ascended masters and their teachings. Specifically, a student of more than ordinary self-discipline and devotion initiated by an ascended master and serving the cause of the Great White Brotherhood.

2. The teaching of Gautama Buddha on attaining nirvana through rightness of knowledge, aspiration, speech, behavior, livelihood, effort, mindfulness, and absorption.

3. The chain of individualized beings fulfilling aspects of God's infinite selfhood. Hierarchy is the means whereby God in the Great Central Sun steps down the energies of his consciousness, that succeeding evolutions in time and space might come to know the wonder of his love.

4. Sanskrit for action or deed. Karma is (1) energy in action; (2) the law of cause and effect and retribution. "Whatsoever a man soweth, that shall he also reap." (Gal. 6:7) Thus the law of karma decrees that from lifetime to lifetime man determines his fate by his actions, including his thoughts, feelings, words, and deeds.

5. The fraternity of saints, sages, and ascended masters of all ages who, coming from every nation, race, and religion, have reunited with the Spirit of the living God and who comprise the heavenly hosts. The term "white" refers to the halo of white light that surrounds their forms. The Great White Brotherhood also includes in its ranks certain unascended chelas of the ascended masters.

6. The ascended master El Morya Khan is Lord (Chohan) of the First Ray of God's Will, Chief of the Darjeeling Council of the Great White Brotherhood, founder of The Summit Lighthouse, and teacher and sponsor of the Messengers Mark and Elizabeth Prophet. El Morya was embodied as the Irish poet Thomas Moore, Akbar the Great, Sir Thomas More, Thomas à Becket, King Arthur, and Melchior, one of the three wise men. See also *The Chela and the Path* by El Morya, published by The Summit Lighthouse.

## CHAPTER 2

1. Peripheral existence is a term which refers to living outside or on the periphery of the circle of God's being. It is an existence in the darkness of sensuality and not-being.

2. The Evil One, or Devil-Tempter. As Jesus the Christ was tempted in the wilderness by the Devil, so Gautama the Buddha was tempted by Mara under the bo tree prior to his enlightenment.

3. Ancient retreat of the Brotherhood established prior to the coming of Sanat Kumara, the Ancient of Days, where the principle focus of the threefold flame of love, wisdom, and power is sustained for all souls evolving upon the planet. When Sanat Kumara returned to Venus on January 1, 1956, Gautama Buddha succeeded him as Lord of the World. From Shamballa in the etheric plane over the Gobi Desert, Gautama Buddha continues to nourish the threefold flame that is the spark of life anchored in the heart chakra of every son and daughter of God and every child of God.

## CHAPTER 3

1. There are fourteen scenes of the last hours of Jesus' life which represent his mastery and sacrifice on behalf of mankind. They are called the fourteen stations of the cross and signify the initiation of the crucifixion, which is passed both on an individual and planetary basis, according to the law of cycles. First station: Jesus is condemned to death; second station: Jesus is made to bear his cross; third station: Jesus falls the first time; fourth station: Jesus meets his afflicted mother; fifth station: Simon the Cyrenian helps Jesus; sixth station: Veronica wipes the face of Jesus; seventh station: Jesus falls the second time; eighth station: Jesus consoles the holy women; ninth station: Jesus falls the third time; tenth station: Jesus is stripped of his garments; eleventh station: Jesus is nailed to the cross; twelfth station: Jesus dies on the cross; thirteenth station: Jesus is taken down from the cross; fourteenth station: Jesus is laid in the sepulcher.

2. The seven rays of the white light which emerge through the prism of the Christ consciousness are (1) blue, (2) yellow, (3) pink, (4) white, (5) green, (6) purple and gold, and (7) violet. There are also five "secret rays" which emerge from the white-fire core of being.

## CHAPTER 4

1. Sanskrit for law. The realization of the law of selfhood through adherence to cosmic law, including the laws of nature and a spiritual code of conduct such as the way or dharma of the Buddha or the Christ. One's duty to fulfill one's raison d'être through the law of love and the sacred labor.

2. Mighty Cosmos is a being who has attained cosmic consciousness and ensouls the energies of many worlds and systems of worlds within this galaxy and beyond with the power of the secret rays.

3. Sanskrit for internal sense organ. The web of life. The net of light

spanning Spirit and Matter connecting and sensitizing the whole of creation within itself and to the heart of God.

4. Base-of-the-spine chakra.

## CHAPTER 5

1. Luke 11:9.

2. The third and fourth perfections of the law are for the mastery of the masculine and the feminine aspects respectively of the second secret ray.

## CHAPTER 7

1. The Messenger Mark L. Prophet. Since his ascension on February 26, 1973, he is known as the ascended master Lanello.

## CHAPTER 8

1. Archangel Michael serves on the first ray of God's will with his divine complement, Archeia Faith. An archangel is an angel who has passed certain advanced initiations qualifying him to preside over lesser angels and bands of angels. Each of the seven rays has an archangel who, with his divine complement, presides over the angels serving on that ray. See p. 137 for a decree to invoke the protection of Archangel Michael through the science of the spoken Word. This science, which has been practiced for many centuries by adepts in the Far East and by Western mystics as well, outlines the uses of the voice in conjunction with the throat chakra in the giving of mantras, prayers, invocations, and decrees. The decree is the most powerful of all applications to the Godhead. It is the command of the son or daughter of God made in the name of the I AM Presence and the Christ for the will of the Almighty to come into manifestation as above, so below. It is the means whereby the kingdom of God becomes a reality here and now through the power of the spoken Word. It may be short or long and usually is marked by a formal preamble and a closing, or acceptance. An explanation of decrees and how they work is given in *The Science of the Spoken Word* by Mark and Elizabeth Prophet, published by The Summit Lighthouse. A complete selection of decrees and songs is available in *Invocations and Decrees for Keepers of the Flame* and *The Summit Lighthouse Book of Songs*.

## CHAPTER 9

1. The ascended master Saint Germain was embodied as Christopher Columbus. He is Lord (Chohan) of the Seventh Ray, hierarch of the Aquarian age, and patron of the United States of America. Saint Germain was accorded the title of "God of Freedom" because of his intense devotion to the flame of freedom and his attainment of the cosmic conscious-

ness of that flame. He was also embodied as Francis Bacon, Merlin, Joseph, the protector of Jesus and Mary, and the prophet Samuel.

2. 1 Cor. 13:7.

## CHAPTER 10

1. Rev. 11:7.

2. Luke 12:2-3.

## CHAPTER 11

1. Rev. 3:11.

## CHAPTER 12

1. In his annual New Year's Eve address given at the Royal Teton Retreat, Gautama Buddha releases the thought form for the year to members of the hierarchy and certain unascended chelas. He also addresses disciples on several planes from a valley of the Himalayas each year at the Wesak Festival at the time of the full moon of Taurus in May. As the flame of Gautama encompasses the earth, all of life receives his blessing, including angels, elementals, and souls walking the path of individual Christhood. The birthday of Gautama Buddha is also celebrated in the flame of Taurus on May 8.

2. On April 16, 1975, Lucifer was bound by Archangel Michael and taken to the Court of the Sacred Fire on Sirius, where he stood trial before the Four and Twenty Elders over a period of ten days. The testimony of many souls of light in embodiment on Terra and other planets and systems in the galaxy were heard, together with that of the ascended masters, archangels, and Elohim. On April 26, 1975, he was found guilty of total rebellion against Almighty God by the unanimous vote of the Twenty Four and sentenced to the second death. As he stood on the disc of the sacred fire before the court, the flame of Alpha and Omega rose as a spiral of intense white light, canceling out an identity and a consciousness that had influenced the fall of one third of the angels of the galaxy and countless lifewaves evolving in this and other systems of worlds.

For information on The Summit Lighthouse, Church Universal and Triumphant, and conferences and seminars conducted by Elizabeth Clare Prophet, write to:

Box A
Colorado Springs, CO 80901

or contact any of the following centers:

Church Universal and Triumphant
International Headquarters
Summit University
Montessori International
1539 East Howard Street
Pasadena, CA 91104

Church Universal and Triumphant
Retreat of the Resurrection Spiral
First and Broadmoor
Colorado Springs, CO 80906

Church Universal and Triumphant
Keepers of the Flame Motherhouse
2112 Santa Barbara Street
Santa Barbara, CA 93105

Church Universal and Triumphant
Los Angeles Community
Teaching Center
1130 Arlington Avenue
Los Angeles, CA 90019

Church Universal and Triumphant
San Francisco Community
Teaching Center
P.O. Box 27463
San Francisco, CA 94127

Church Universal and Triumphant
Boulder Community Teaching Center
P.O. Box 3571
Boulder, CO 80303

Church Universal and Triumphant
Minneapolis/St. Paul Community
Teaching Center
1206 Fifth Street SE
Minneapolis, MN 55414

Church Universal and Triumphant
Chicago Community Teaching Center
P.O. Box 5148
Chicago, IL 60680

Church Universal and Triumphant
New York City Community
Teaching Center
P.O. Box 667
Lenox Hill Station
New York, NY 10021

Church Universal and Triumphant
Washington, D.C. Community
Teaching Center
4715 Sixteenth Street NW
Washington, D.C. 20011

You are invited to study the teachings of the ascended masters published by The Summit Lighthouse as *Pearls of Wisdom* and sent to you on a love-offering basis. For information write to:

> The Summit Lighthouse
> Box A
> Colorado Springs, CO 80901

For information on Summit University write to:

> Summit University
> Box A
> Colorado Springs, CO 80901